SECOND EDITION

THE 4-INGREDIENT DIABETES COOKBOOK

NANCY S. HUGHES

SIMPLE, QUICK AND DELICIOUS RECIPES USING JUST FOUR INGREDIENTS OR LESS!

Director, Book Publishing, Abe Ogden; *Managing Editor, Project Manager*, Rebekah Renshaw; *Acquisitions Editor*, Victor Van Beuren; *Production Manager*, Melissa Sprott; *Composition*, Circle Graphics; *Cover Design*, Jody Billert, Design Literate Studio; *Photography*, Tara Donne Photography; *Printer*, Versa Press.

Printed in the United States of America
3 5 7 9 10 8 6 4 2

The suggestions and information contained in this publication are generally consistent with the *Standards of Medical Care in Diabetes* and other policies of the American Diabetes Association, but they do not represent the policy or position of the Association or any of its boards or committees. Reasonable steps have been taken to ensure the accuracy of the information presented. However, the American Diabetes Association cannot ensure the safety or efficacy of any product or service described in this publication. Individuals are advised to consult a physician or other appropriate health care professional before undertaking any diet or exercise program or taking any medication referred to in this publication. Professionals must use and apply their own professional judgment, experience, and training and should not rely solely on the information contained in this publication before prescribing any diet, exercise, or medication. The American Diabetes Association—its officers, directors, employees, volunteers, and members—assumes no responsibility or liability for personal or other injury, loss, or damage that may result from the suggestions or information in this publication.

♾ The paper in this publication meets the requirements of the ANSI Standard Z39.48-1992 (permanence of paper).

ADA titles may be purchased for business or promotional use or for special sales. To purchase more than 50 copies of this book at a discount, or for custom editions of this book with your logo, contact the American Diabetes Association at the address below or at booksales@diabetes.org.

American Diabetes Association
1701 North Beauregard Street
Alexandria, Virginia 22311

DOI: 10.2337/9781580406376

Library of Congress Cataloging-in-Publication Data

Names: Hughes, Nancy S., author.
Title: The 4-ingredient diabetes cookbook : simple, quick and delicious
  recipes using just four ingredients or less! / Nancy S. Hughes.
Other titles: Four ingredient diabetes cookbook
Description: 2nd ed. | Alexandria : American Diabetes Association, [2016]
Identifiers: LCCN 2016013301 | ISBN 9781580406376 (paperback)
Subjects: LCSH: Diabetes--Diet therapy--Recipes. | BISAC: COOKING / Health &
  Healing / Diabetic & Sugar-Free. | COOKING / Health & Healing / Heart. |
  COOKING / Methods / Quick & Easy. | COOKING / Health & Healing / Weight
  Control.
Classification: LCC RC662 .H83 2016 | DDC 641.5/6314--dc23
LC record available at https://lccn.loc.gov/2016013301

CONTENTS

DEDICATION

To My Husband, Greg

For your endless support and your even-more-endless taste-testing abilities ...
you are always there for me!

Double-Duty Banana Pancakes

page 36

ACKNOWLEDGMENTS

My family, Greg, Will, Kelly, Molly, Anna Flynn, Sully, Annie, Terry, Jilli, Jesse, Emma, Lucy, Taft, and Kara . . . for simply surviving in this culinary swirl of life!

My editor, Rebekah Renshaw, for your quick responses, your positive feedback, and your sound advice . . . oh, and the occasional fun dinner in city after city!

Melanie McKibbon, my business manager, my right/left arm . . . you can always find my head even under a pile of papers!

Sylvia Vollmer, my kitchen "all-purpose" wonder, my shopper, chopper, and everything in between . . . thanks for always being there for me!

Southwestern Protein
Powered Bowls

page 120

Introduction

4 Ingredients... REALLY????

Yes! This book is for people with diabetes—and for those who want to eat healthier simply, who don't want to "live" in the kitchen! Inside you'll find more than 160 delicious recipes, all made with four ingredients or less! (In case you're checking up on me, salt, pepper, water, and cooking spray don't count as ingredients, and I counted the zest and juice of the same fruit as one ingredient.) Some of these recipes even call for three or only two ingredients, and still taste scrumptious.

Just stop and think about it. Using fewer ingredients can simplify your life and _ease_ your workload tremendously! It means fewer items in your grocery cart, less time in the grocery line, fewer items to unload and put away when you get home, less time to prepare the dish, and, the best thing—fewer pots and pans to scrub! You'll actually have time to do... well, anything else you want, because you won't be stuck in the kitchen (or in the grocery store) all the time!

I consider myself a lazy cook. I'm always looking for that shorter cut, that quicker way, anything to help me avoid work but, at the same time, I want my efforts to count.

So I created more than 160 recipes that use only 4 ingredients, meet the American Diabetes Association's nutritional standards, and are jam-packed with flavor. I'll admit that it was a definite challenge. Even though I've been developing quick and healthy recipes for over 25 years, it was still tricky, but I felt there was a need. I wanted to introduce a fresh approach to people whose lives may already be burdened with numbers, counting, and chores.

I wanted to show people how to discover that simpler is better, and faster can be more delicious, when every ingredient really counts. The secret, I found, is not the number of ingredients, but rather the different types of ingredients and the various techniques included in the recipes. For example, by using highly flavored ingredients and convenience foods that contain several ingredients in one product, such as picante sauce or herb blends, I can shorten the ingredient list drastically without compromising on flavor. As for effective techniques, something as simple as searing or reducing ingredients (that is, cooking them down to a more concentrated form over high heat) is an extremely easy, fast way to get intense flavor without adding extra ingredients, fat, or time.

If the meal prep is simple and the great flavors are still there, those same healthy recipes will be made over and over again . . . because they're "doable" AND "delicious"!! That's my whole point in writing this book: to help people with diabetes stay on a healthy track all the time, bringing them tons of flavor and fresh new ideas that will be used a lifetime. My no-hassle approach is just that . . . easy and approachable, so that everyone can have the "I can do THAT!" attitude.

The American Diabetes Association is a trusted, reliable, highly respected health organization and together, we've done the work for you. You _can_ trust that all of these recipes are good for you and meet their standards. We've given you all the numbers to help you monitor your intake of fat, sodium, and carb. You don't have to worry if the recipes are "okay" for you. You can enjoy eating again without the math swirling in your head all the time . . . and with a fraction of the work!

I hope you're hungry!

Enjoy,

Kitchen Tools You'll Really Use

Besides the usual pots, pans, cookie sheets, measuring cups, and slotted spoons, there are certain items that make cooking faster and easier. They help keep me from overheating or underheating a skillet, burning a sauce, and basically ruining a lot of recipes!

Fine grater. This is also known as a microplane. It's great for zesting (that is, grating the peel from a citrus fruit) and finely grating hard cheeses, fresh gingerroot, and even garlic. It's made of stainless steel that has been perforated with sharp-edged, small holes. Buy the variety that is made of stainless steel, rather than tin, so it won't rust. Also, choose the style that has a rubber handle or grip at the top for better control. A fine grater makes grating easy and effortless!

Garlic press. This tool is used to press a garlic clove through tiny holes, which extracts both the pulp and the juice. I think so much more garlic flavor is released using a garlic press than with chopping because pressing produces a finer texture and the oils and flavors are not absorbed into the cutting board. You can place a small or medium clove in the garlic press without peeling it, then press down. The meat of the garlic comes through, leaving behind the peel! Larger cloves of garlic need to be halved first. (And here's a bizarre garlic tip for you: to neutralize the garlic aroma on your fingertips, wash your hands, then run your fingertips over any chrome you may have, such as your faucet or towel bar. The aroma magically disappears! You have to try this and see for yourself.)

Gravy or fat separator. This removes grease from hot cooking liquid. It is a small, clear pitcher made of glass or heatproof plastic. You pour the hot liquid into the pitcher and allow it to stand for 2 to 3 minutes, and the fat will rise to the top. The pitcher is designed so that the liquid can be poured out, leaving the grease behind.

Small fine-mesh sieve. This helps you strain or deseed raspberries or anything with small bits or pieces that need to be removed. Use it for sifting small amounts of powdered sugar evenly over cakes and cookies, too.

Hand-held wooden reamer. This is used for juicing citrus fruits, such as lemons, limes, and oranges. It is a ridged, teardrop-shaped tool with a handle. Simply cut the fruit in half crosswise and press it into the point of the reamer. Twist the reamer back and forth to extract the juices. You get so much more juice out of the fruit than you could by simply squeezing it with your hands.

Kitchen scale. The scales in the produce aisles aren't always accurate, and sometimes it's hard to divide out the correct amount of meat and seafood you need for any given recipe. The best way to be accurate is to weigh it on your own scales. Buy the variety with a removable tray so it can go in the dishwasher or be cleaned easily. You'll be surprised how often you use it.

Metal or plastic ruler. Yep, I'm not kidding. Use one to accurately measure ingredients that need to be cut into 1-inch cubes, 1/2-inch wedges, or 2-inch strips. You'll soon learn how to do this without measuring, and your cooking results will be more successful if your same-sized ingredients cook evenly.

Mini muffin tins. These are a fraction of the standard size, but you will feel more satisfied if you bake your muffins and quick breads in them because you can have more than one! They're nice to serve when entertaining, too. Try making mini quiches with them—great for a brunch buffet table.

Paper towels. Yes, a paper towel can be a very functional tool, beyond drying your hands and cleaning up spills. Use a damp paper towel to wipe mushrooms clean, to pat chicken or fish dry before cooking, to aid in removing the skin from chicken (it provides the traction needed), and—my personal favorite—when you put a couple of damp paper towels under a cutting board, they keep the cutting board in place instead of slipping and sliding around!

Silicone spatulas. These are basically rubber spatulas that can stand the heat. Use them with nonstick skillets and saucepans to scrape their bottoms and sides, collecting all of the concentrated flavors that accumulate there while cooking. They are also gentler on ingredients when stirring and tossing and prevent the ingredients from breaking down too much. Buy several different sizes to keep on hand.

Vegetable peeler with a rubber handle. You may already have your favorite kind of vegetable peeler, but I love this variety because, more times than not, I have wet hands when working in the kitchen, and the rubber handle keeps them from slipping—which makes it a lot faster to get the job done. To make the job go even faster, peel the vegetables under running water. The peeling slips away into the garbage disposal as you peel. There's another step saved!

Pull, Prep, and Preheat

Before you actually start to cook a recipe, you can do a few things to make the process go even more smoothly.

Pull the ingredients. This sounds obvious, but you'd be surprised how much faster you can cook if you pull everything you need out of the pantry and fridge and line it up on the counter before you start.

Prep the ingredients. Then, start prepping everything you need according to the ingredient list. Have all items prepped before you start following the recipe directions. For example, if the ingredient reads, "1/2 cup chopped onion" or "1 pound boneless sirloin steak, trimmed of fat and cut into 1-inch cubes," have that done before you start the first step. Most of my recipes cook so quickly, you really don't have enough time to chop the onion while the steak cubes are browning.

Preheat the skillet. When a recipe calls for heating the skillet "until hot" before adding ingredients, how can you tell if it's hot enough? An electric range takes about 2 minutes to properly heat a pan. Set your new digital timer so you don't overheat the pan. Or use the time-honored "pancake test": sprinkle a few drops of water in the pan. If they "dance" or bounce vigorously, the pan's hot!

Make the Most of All Your Meals

BREAKFAST

Cereal. Toast. Cereal. Toast. It can get pretty monotonous. Get out of your rut! Take a new approach toward the breakfast meal and what it has to offer.

With our multitasking day and night, why not set the breakfast meal to multitasking, too? Serve these tasty recipes not only for breakfast, but also for lunch, midday snack, dinner, and even dessert.

Or take a look in the other chapters, such as Beverages or Snacks, and see what would work for a breakfast item. Just choose the recipes to fit your inclinations, while keeping track of your carb intake. I designed these recipes to be versatile enough to fit into other parts of your day as well, giving you even more choices for each meal.

BREAKFAST TRICKS, TIPS, AND TIMESAVERS

Bake a batch. Muffins or quick breads are perfect for breakfast for one day and a snack or dessert the next. Then freeze the rest in small baggies and pull them out when you need them.

Breakfast power drinks. You can make the beverage recipes in this chapter in just a few minutes, making them great additions to your "on the run" meal or "computer" lunch. Since you need power all day, why not feel as though you're having a treat while you're at it?

Double-time your meals. Make a batch of breakfast-grilled sandwiches, have one for breakfast, and refrigerate the rest. Pop one into the microwave at work or home the next day for a quick "already-made" lunch.

Add a veggie or salad. For dinner, all you need is to steam a few vegetables and toss a fruit salad to transform an omelet or frittata into a fast-fixing dinner option.

Reverse it. Make a fruit drink from the Beverage chapter for breakfast. A fruit drink has fruit juices, fruit, and sometimes yogurt in it ... make one a fun and easy part of your breakfast! Or how about using the skillet-grilled fruit in the Fruit Sides chapter to serve alongside your turkey sausage or Canadian bacon in the morning. It's easy to expand your menu once you start thinking out of the breakfast box.

SNACKS

Portion control is key with snacks and appetizers! It's easier to keep a handle on things when you're in your own home, but when you're at a family gathering or attending a big event, the array of foods spread out before you can be a bit mind boggling. Two things you can do to make it easy on yourself: have a light snack before you go, and don't socialize too close to the buffet table. The light snack will help in curbing your appetite, so you won't be starving when you get there. Keeping your conversations away from the table will prevent you from mindlessly munching while you're visiting. Fix a small plate and move to another area to focus in on your friends, old and new, and have some fun!

SNACK TRICKS, TIPS, AND TIMESAVERS

Crunch without crackers. Take a nice break from serving crackers or chips with dip or spreads—try crostini instead. Crostini is a fancy name for little toasted and cooled bread slices. Using baguette bread (the skinny loaf) is your best bet—simply slice, bake briefly, and cool. It's much cheaper than those expensive crackers and chips, too!

Spread it out. Stretch those strong-flavored cheeses as far as they can go by combining a small amount of them with fat-free cream cheese or sour cream. Then add to dips or spreads.

Accent the cheese. Add fresh herbs, such as basil or cilantro, to seasoned light cheese spreads, fat-free cream cheese, or fat-free sour cream, to give tons of flavor in every bite.

Small bites need heat. Add a touch of heat, whether it's with dried pepper flakes, cayenne pepper, chipotle chilis, jalapeño peppers, or hot pepper sauce. The heat intensifies the other flavors in the dish—but remember, a little goes a long way!

Fresh is best. When making fresh salsas, whether they're fruit- or vegetable-based, it's best to serve them within a couple of hours after tossing the ingredients together... otherwise they tend to lose those peak, distinct flavors and become more mellow and blended.

SALADS

There's tossed salads, arranged salads, fruit salads, vegetable-based salads, pasta salads, main dish salads, and potato salads. Use your imagination when making salads—go beyond the bag of greens and a bottle of salad dressing. They're okay in a pinch, but there's a lot more you can do with a salad with little effort and very little fat.

SALAD TRICKS, TIPS, AND TIMESAVERS

Less dressing, more flavor. Hold off on some of that dressing and add small amounts of flavorful ingredients instead, such as feta or Parmesan cheese, artichoke hearts, olives, lean ham or turkey pepperoni, and, of course, fresh herbs.

Think small tomatoes. You can always rely on those little sweet grape tomatoes for that year-round, peak-season flavor. They're packed with concentrated flavors that burst with sweetness. Cut them in half to make the flavors (and your dollar) go twice as far!

Cut the mayo. But hang on to flavor and texture.

- Replace part of the mayonnaise with fat-free sour cream.
- Use a reduced-fat creamy salad dressing, such as ranch, for pasta- and potato-based salads. Be sure to incorporate other highly flavored ingredients, such as onion or green peppers, to balance flavor and texture.
- Add low-fat buttermilk to your mayo-based salad dressings. It adds thickness and gives a lift to the other ingredient flavors while tying everything together.

Toast those nuts. Even if it's just 2 tablespoons of nuts, the nutty flavor will travel so much further if you toast them ... and it takes just 2 minutes in a hot skillet.

Ditch the seeds. Tomatoes and cucumbers are often seeded in recipes. It's an important step—don't skip it. Removing the seeds prevents the dish from getting too much liquid in it and diluting the other flavors.

- There are two ways to seed a tomato. First, halve the tomato crosswise (that's parallel to the stem portion of the tomato) and squeeze the juices and seeds out; or halve the tomato the same way, then place your clean fingertips in the seed pockets. The juices and seeds will rise to the surface and you can push them out.
- To seed a cucumber, cut it in half lengthwise, and run the tip of a teaspoon down the center to scrape the seeds out easily.

Shake and serve. Bottled ingredients, particularly soy sauce, Worcestershire sauce, and, of course, salad dressings, really do need to be shaken before using. I know that sounds a bit elementary, but it does make a big difference.

SOUPS

Soup makes a perfect partner for salads and sandwiches. It can bring much-needed comfort after a hard day, or act as a special first course when you're entertaining. But did you know that soup can be loaded with sodium, bankrupt of nutrition, and exploding with fat and carb? Be careful when you're in a restaurant or grabbing a couple of cans from your grocer's shelves. Ask questions, read labels, and think twice before you order. The soups in this book are worry-free and packed with flavor and nutrition...all the good things that should be connected with the soup you eat!

SOUP TRICKS, TIPS, AND TIMESAVERS

Stock up. Keep a variety of frozen vegetables and vegetable combinations stored away to make a quick soup any time you feel like it. One of my favorite quick veggie items to add to soups is the pepper stir-fry, which contains multicolored pepper strips and onion. It's so versatile, and there's no chopping needed—that's the good part! Keep in mind, though, that the onions in the stir-fry take longer to cook than other vegetables, about 20 minutes.

Thaw frozen vegetables quickly. Place them in a colander and run under cold water 20 to 30 seconds, then shake off excess liquid before continuing with the recipe.

Keep those veggies coming. Keep a resealable quart- or gallon-sized freezer bag in your freezer. Every time you have a few leftover veggies, toss them into the bag—in no time, you'll have enough to make soup! Keep a can of stewed tomatoes and some chicken broth on hand to make soup any time you feel like some.

Rinse canned beans. To remove the thick liquid and some of the sodium, place the beans in a colander, run under cold water, and shake off excess liquid before continuing with the recipe.

Make it thick. No need to add flour or cornstarch. Just use a hand mixer to puree 1 to 1 1/2 cups of the soup, or use a blender and puree until smooth, then return the thick mixture to the saucepot. (It's very important to hold the blender lid down tightly before you turn it on, or your soup will fly everywhere!)

Make it fresh. If you want to add a bit of fresh flavor to your soup, serve it topped with a sprinkling of fresh parsley, green onion, or any fresh herb that is already in the soup.

Bring out the cheese. Reserve a tablespoon or two of the cheese that's supposed to go into the soup and sprinkle it on top at serving time. That enhances a soup's cheesy flavor without increasing calories or fat.

Heat it up. Add some spicy heat in the form of dried red pepper flakes or a little hot pepper sauce just before serving—your soups will taste fuller and more substantial. A little heat goes a long way, so be sure to start with a tiny bit—you can always add more!

MAIN DISHES

Seasonings play a very important part in main dishes. It's important how and when you use them. To get the most flavor from your meats and casseroles, sometimes you need to season before you start to cook, and other times, after. Check the tips below for some great seasoning ideas.

MAIN DISH TRICKS, TIPS, AND TIMESAVERS

Season with the skin on. Season a chicken or turkey that will be cooked with the skin on by lifting up the skin and rubbing the seasonings between the meat and the skin. Then roast the bird. The seasonings will penetrate into the meat of the bird rather than get lost in the skin that is discarded.

Check the label. Some brands of turkey breast and pork tenderloin have broth or solution added, which means added sodium. Be sure to read the package labels, and if the turkey or pork does contain broth or solution, don't add more salt when cooking it.

Use coffee granules. If you haven't tried using coffee to intensify the hearty flavor of beef, you'll be amazed! Just add 1/2 cup of strong coffee to the roasting pan and pop it in the oven. Or use instant coffee granules dissolved in water. And you don't need to heat the liquid first—the granules dissolve in either hot or cold liquid. Just be sure to stir them well.

Deepen the color. To give a deeper brown appearance to pork, beef, poultry, or fish, dust with a small amount of paprika or chili powder before cooking. Just a light sprinkle will give more color than flavor.

Crush those herbs. Dried herbs take a longer time to release their flavors than fresh or ground varieties, so crush the dried herb leaves between your fingertips before adding them to the dish. Fresh herb flavors are strong, but they fade quickly if cooked for a long time.

Use citrus zest and juice. When a recipe calls for both the zest and juice of a lemon, lime, or orange, always grate the piece of fruit first before squeezing the juice out. It's easier to grate when the fruit is full and firm. Grate only the colorful part of the fruit, not the white pith underneath—that gives the dish a bitter taste.

MAIN DISH TRICKS, TIPS, AND TIMESAVERS AFTER YOU START COOKING

Add ground spices. If you need a stronger, more intense flavor in a dish, add ground spices after cooking. You just need a small amount, and the flavor doesn't break down while cooking.

Use a smidgen of sugar. Add small amounts (1/2 to 1 teaspoon) to stews and skillet dishes. It doesn't add sweetness to the dish, but aids in cutting the acidity of the other ingredients and acts to blend the flavors together.

A so-simple sauce. Reduction is a fancy word for boiling down the liquid in a dish quickly to leave a deeply flavored, intense sauce. This is my favorite cooking trick. Simply add water, broth, or wine to the skillet after sautéing other ingredients. The liquid will absorb the concentrated seasonings that build up in the skillet during the cooking process, then boil down in 1 or 2 minutes to create a quick, highly flavored sauce.

Last-minute flavors. Add the following ingredients to your dishes once they have been removed from the heat. These can also be added to cold entrees at serving time.

- Extracts, such as vanilla and almond extract
- Grated citrus rind and gingerroot
- Flavored oils, such as extra virgin olive oil and sesame oil
- Toasted nuts

STARCHY SIDES

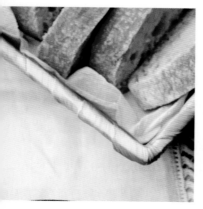

Most nutrition experts will agree that all forms of carb can be okay if you eat them in moderation. But if you ask me, starchy sides are one of the hardest food categories to control. The carb in them can creep up on you if you're not careful. By choosing the right starchy sides and using some of the tricks below, though, you can enjoy them and feel like you've had a large portion without going overboard.

STARCHY SIDE TRICKS, TIPS, AND TIMESAVERS

Bulk it up. Add low-carb vegetables and fruits to a starchy dish to add volume, giving you the feeling that you're eating more than you actually are. This not only adds character to a humdrum side dish, but sneaks in extra vitamins as well. For example, bulk up pasta by tossing in fresh or frozen veggies during the last few minutes of cooking.

Break it in thirds. When using spaghetti noodles as a side, break them in thirds so they are easier to serve and combine better with the vegetables in the dish.

Hollow it out. Heat French bread in the oven, then hollow out the center and use the outer portion for crunchy sandwiches. Save the insides for bread crumbs or croutons—and save some calories, too.

Serve it thin. Instead of a huge hunk of French bread with dinner, bake thin slices of French bread, let them cool slightly, and rub a halved garlic clove lightly over each piece. The larger number of smaller pieces, the delicious crunchiness, and the rich garlic taste will satisfy you well before you eat too much.

Sub in some cauliflower. Cut the amount of potatoes used in your favorite soup recipe by half and substitute with an equal amount of cauliflower. Cauliflower provides great potato-like texture and appearance with much less carb. Try serving mashed cauliflower instead of potatoes.

VEGETABLE SIDES

Night after night of boiled frozen veggies, or heated canned ones, can get really tiresome. The recipes here let you see how easy, interesting, and sensational veggie and fruit sides can be. By preparing them in a variety of ways—roasted, steamed, stuffed, mixed with other vegetables, skillet-grilled, and more—you'll look at vegetable sides in a different light... and find some new favorites.

VEGETABLE TRICKS, TIPS, AND TIMESAVERS

Line it with foil. When roasting vegetables, always line the baking sheet with foil to protect the baking sheet surface and give you easy clean-up.

Maximize your buttery taste. To get the most concentrated "butter" flavors from light margarine—whether you boil, steam, or roast the veggies—add it after cooking, not during. And don't worry about melting light margarine first—just place it directly on the veggies and let their heat melt it. The flavor of light margarine is so much better that way.

The right cut. How you cut a vegetable is important, so be sure to follow the recipe's instructions. Veggie cut affects the evenness of cooking, cooking time, and recipe presentation, so follow directions to be successful!

DESSERTS

Here is where choosing the right carb can really make the most difference. By using lower-fat versions of cream cheese, ice cream, and yogurt; by including plenty of fresh fruits, berries, and melons; and by choosing truly delicious recipes to prepare, you'll end up with a scrumptious, decent-sized dessert on your plate—and you'll be satisfied without wanting to overindulge. These recipes and the tricks below help you have the sweet stuff—the cakes, pies, parfaits, and icecream desserts—without going out of bounds.

DESSERT TRICKS, TIPS, AND TIMESAVERS

Have your snack cake and eat it, too. You can make your own snack cakes quickly and easily from boxed cake mixes. Simply add fruit—any fruit you like, either mashed or the jarred baby food version—instead of oil and cook the cake a few minutes less. To see if your snack cake is done, test it with a wooden toothpick. When the toothpick comes out almost clean, the cake's done. It will continue to cook while cooling and will stay moist.

Stretch your snack cake. Bake the snack cake batter in mini muffin tins but cook them a few minutes less. These little cakes are great for a midmorning snack or a brown bag lunch.

Rev up the chocolate flavor. Add a bit of instant coffee granules to chocolate cake mixes and brownie mixes for a deeper chocolatey flavor.

Sweeten fruit-based desserts. Use all-fruit spreads instead of sugar. Heat the fruit spread briefly in the microwave to melt it slightly, and then toss it with your favorite fruit or add it to your favorite recipe.

Make a mini pie. Make individual tarts using refrigerated piecrust, cutting rounds with a biscuit cutter and baking in muffin tins. Serve them with a spoonful of sugar-free whipped topping and overflowing with fresh fruit.

BEVERAGES

Pineapple Apricot Fizz

SERVES 8 ■ **SERVING SIZE** 1/2 cup ■ **PREP TIME** 5 minutes

2 cups cold pineapple juice
(or pineapple, orange, and
banana juice blend)

1 cup cold apricot nectar

2 cups diet ginger ale

1 Combine the juice and nectar in a pitcher and stir.
Pour into 4 tall glasses with ice.

2 Add 1/4 cup ginger ale to each serving and stir gently
to blend. Serve immediately.

EXCHANGES / CHOICES

1 Fruit

Calories	50
Calories from Fat	0
Total Fat	**0.0 g**
Saturated Fat	0.0 g
Trans Fat	0.0 g
Cholesterol	0 mg
Sodium	0 mg
Potassium	120 mg
Total Carbohydrate	13 g
Dietary Fiber	0 g
Sugars	10 g
Protein	0 g
Phosphorus	10 mg

COOK'S TIP

Be sure to shake the nectar well before you measure! For
more fizz, add 1/4 cup additional ginger ale to each serving.

Cappuccino Chiller

SERVES 4 ■ **SERVING SIZE** 1/2 cup ■ **PREP TIME** 5 minutes

2 cups fat-free, sugar-free vanilla
   ice cream

1 cup water

1 tablespoon instant coffee granules

4 ice cubes or 1/2 cup coarsely
   crushed ice

1 Place all ingredients in a blender and blend until smooth.

2 Sweeten to taste with pourable sugar substitute.

EXCHANGES / CHOICES
1 1/2 Carbohydrate

Calories	80
Calories from Fat	0
Total Fat	0.0 g
Saturated Fat	0.0 g
Trans Fat	0.0 g
Cholesterol	5 mg
Sodium	65 mg
Potassium	210 mg
Total Carbohydrate	20 g
Dietary Fiber	5 g
Sugars	5 g
Protein	4 g
Phosphorus	55 mg

COOK'S TIP
This recipe easily doubles, but make it in two batches for easier blending.

Tropical Strawberry Cream

SERVES 3 ■ **SERVING SIZE** 1 cup ■ **PREP TIME** 4 minutes

1 cup fat-free, artificially sweetened, vanilla-flavored yogurt

1 1/4 cups whole strawberries, stems removed

1/2 ripe medium banana

1 (6-ounce) can pineapple juice

1 Place all ingredients in a blender and blend until smooth.

EXCHANGES / CHOICES

1 Fruit
1/2 Milk, fat-free

Calories	100
Calories from Fat	5
Total Fat	0.5 g
Saturated Fat	0.1 g
Trans Fat	0.0 g
Cholesterol	0 mg
Sodium	35 mg
Potassium	350 mg
Total Carbohydrate	23 g
Dietary Fiber	2 g
Sugars	16 g
Protein	3 g
Phosphorus	90 mg

COOK'S TIP

You can make this recipe up to 24 hours before serving.

Cranberry-Splashed Ginger Tea

SERVES 4 ■ **SERVING SIZE** 1 cup ■ **PREP TIME** 5 minutes ■ **STAND TIME** 30 minutes

3 cups water

2 tea bags

4 (2-inch-long) gingerroot pieces, peeled

1 cup artificially sweetened cranberry juice cocktail

2–3 tablespoons pourable sugar substitute

1. Bring the water to a boil in a medium saucepan over high heat. Remove from the heat, add tea bags and gingerroot, and steep for 2 minutes.

2. Remove the tea bags. Let the gingerroot and tea stand for 30 minutes.

3. Pour the tea and gingerroot into a small pitcher, add the juice and sugar substitute, and stir until blended. Refrigerate until needed, then remove ginger and serve over ice.

EXCHANGES / CHOICES
Free Food

Calories	15
Calories from Fat	0
Total Fat	0.0 g
Saturated Fat	0.0 g
Trans Fat	0.0 g
Cholesterol	0 mg
Sodium	15 mg
Potassium	90 mg
Total Carbohydrate	4 g
Dietary Fiber	0 g
Sugars	3 g
Protein	0 g
Phosphorus	0 mg

COOK'S TIP
For a stronger ginger flavor, cover the tea with plastic wrap and refrigerate overnight or at least 8 hours.

Sweet Citrus Cooler

SERVES 4 ◼ **SERVING SIZE** 3/4 cup ◼ **PREP TIME** 5 minutes

1 1/2 cups water

1 cup white grape juice

3–4 tablespoons lemon juice

3–4 tablespoons lime juice

3 tablespoons pourable sugar substitute

1 Combine all ingredients in a small pitcher and stir until well blended.

2 Refrigerate until needed.

EXCHANGES / CHOICES
1 Fruit

Calories	50
Calories from Fat	0
Total Fat	0.0 g
Saturated Fat	0.0 g
Trans Fat	0.0 g
Cholesterol	0 mg
Sodium	10 mg
Potassium	100 mg
Total Carbohydrate	12 g
Dietary Fiber	0 g
Sugars	11 g
Protein	0 g
Phosphorus	10 mg

COOK'S TIP
Use fresh lemon and lime juice for peak flavors. One medium lemon or lime yields about 2 tablespoons of juice.

Mocha Power Pickup

2 cups fat-free half-and-half

2 packets (0.53 ounces each) sugar-free
hot cocoa mix

2 tablespoons reduced-fat peanut butter

1/2–1 teaspoon instant coffee granules

1/2 cup ice cubes (optional)

1 Place all ingredients in a blender and blend until smooth.

EXCHANGES / CHOICES

1 Carbohydrate
1/2 Fat

Calories	100
Calories from Fat	25
Total Fat	3.0 g
Saturated Fat	0.9 g
Trans Fat	0.0 g
Cholesterol	5 mg
Sodium	140 mg
Potassium	340 mg
Total Carbohydrate	13 g
Dietary Fiber	1 g
Sugars	6 g
Protein	4 g
Phosphorus	185 mg

COOK'S TIP
Use the ice for a colder drink.

Almond Quinoa with Cranberries
page 28

BREAKFAST

Good Morning Power Parfait

SERVES 4 ■ **SERVING SIZE** 1 parfait ■ **PREP TIME** 5 minutes

1 ripe medium banana

2 cups fat-free, artificially sweetened, vanilla-flavored yogurt (divided use)

1 teaspoon ground cinnamon

1 cup whole strawberries, sliced

1/2 cup grape-nut-style cereal, preferably with raisins and almonds

1 Add the banana, 1 cup yogurt, and 1 teaspoon cinnamon, if desired, to a blender and blend until smooth. Pour into 4 wine or parfait glasses.

2 Top each parfait with 1/4 cup sliced strawberries, 1/4 cup yogurt, and 2 tablespoons cereal.

EXCHANGES / CHOICES

1 Starch
1/2 Fruit
1/2 Milk, fat-free

Calories	140
Calories from Fat	5
Total Fat	0.5 g
Saturated Fat	0.2 g
Trans Fat	0.0 g
Cholesterol	0 mg
Sodium	125 mg
Potassium	390 mg
Total Carbohydrate	32 g
Dietary Fiber	3 g
Sugars	14 g
Protein	5 g
Phosphorus	150 mg

COOK'S TIP

This parfait's a great way to start your day—it's packed with vitamin C and fiber!

Almond Quinoa with Cranberries

SERVES 4 ■ **SERVING SIZE** 1 cup ■ **PREP TIME** 5 minutes ■ **COOK TIME** 17 minutes

4 ounces slivered almonds

3/4 cup dry quinoa

3 tablespoons dried cranberries

1 tablespoon honey (or 1 tablespoon cinnamon sugar)

1. Heat a large saucepan over medium-high heat. Add almonds and cook 2 minutes or until beginning to lightly brown, stirring frequently. Set aside on separate plate.

2. Pour 1 1/2 cups water into the saucepan and bring to a boil, add the quinoa, reduce heat to low, cover and cook 13–15 minutes or until liquid is absorbed. Remove from heat and let stand, covered, for 5 minutes.

3. Top with the almonds and cranberries. Drizzle with the honey (or sprinkle with cinnamon sugar.)

EXCHANGES / CHOICES

2 Starch
1/2 Other carbohydrate
3 Fat

Calories	330
Calories from Fat	140
Total Fat	16 g
Saturated Fat	1.3 g
Trans Fat	0.0 g
Cholesterol	0 mg
Sodium	0 mg
Potassium	385 mg
Total Carbohydrate	39 g
Dietary Fiber	6 g
Sugars	12 g
Protein	11 g
Phosphorus	285 mg

COOK'S TIP

This makes a great side for roast pork or chicken OR as a breakfast side to chicken sausage or Canadian bacon. (If used as a side, it will serve 8; serving size: 1/2 cup.)

Busy Day Breakfast Burrito

SERVES 4 ■ **SERVING SIZE** 1 burrito ■ **PREP TIME** 5 minutes ■ **COOK TIME** 3 minutes

1 1/2 cups egg substitute

4 (6-inch) whole-wheat flour tortillas

1/4 cup fresh, no-salt-added pico de gallo

1/2 cup shredded, reduced-fat, sharp cheddar cheese

1 Place a small nonstick skillet over medium heat until hot. Coat the skillet with nonstick cooking spray, add egg substitute, and cook, without stirring, until egg mixture begins to set on bottom, about 1 minute.

2 Draw a spatula across the bottom of pan to form large curds. Continue cooking until egg mixture is thick but still moist; do not stir constantly.

3 Place the tortillas on a microwave-safe plate and microwave on HIGH for 15 seconds or until heated. Top each with equal amounts of the egg mixture.

4 Spoon 1 tablespoon pico de gallo evenly over the egg on each tortilla, sprinkle with 2 tablespoons cheese, and roll up.

EXCHANGES / CHOICES

1 Starch
2 Protein, lean

Calories	180
Calories from Fat	40
Total Fat	4.5 g
Saturated Fat	2.0 g
Trans Fat	0.0 g
Cholesterol	5 mg
Sodium	450 mg
Potassium	210 mg
Total Carbohydrate	18 g
Dietary Fiber	1 g
Sugars	2 g
Protein	16 g
Phosphorus	125 mg

COOK'S TIP

Use extra-sharp cheddar cheese for a more intense cheese flavor. In general, this is a great way to stretch the cheese flavor in recipes without adding fat or calories.

English Muffin Melts

4 whole-wheat English muffins,
   cut in half

2 tablespoons reduced-fat mayonnaise

3 ounces sliced reduced-fat Swiss
   cheese, torn in small pieces

4 ounces oven-roasted deli turkey,
   finely chopped

1 Preheat the broiler.

2 Arrange the muffin halves on a baking sheet and place under the broiler for 1–2 minutes or until lightly toasted. Remove from broiler and spread 3/4 teaspoon mayonnaise over each muffin half.

3 Arrange the cheese pieces evenly on each muffin half and top with the turkey.

4 Return to the broiler and cook 3 minutes, or until the turkey is just beginning to turn golden and the cheese has melted.

EXCHANGES / CHOICES

1 Starch
1 Protein, lean

Calories	120
Calories from Fat	30
Total Fat	3.5 g
Saturated Fat	1.3 g
Trans Fat	0.0 g
Cholesterol	15 mg
Sodium	290 mg
Potassium	115 mg
Total Carbohydrate	15 g
Dietary Fiber	2 g
Sugars	3 g
Protein	9 g
Phosphorus	185 mg

COOK'S TIP

Be sure to arrange the items in the order suggested—the cheese has a creamier texture when you place it on top of the mayonnaise.

Sweet Onion Frittata with Ham

SERVES 4 ■ **SERVING SIZE** 1/4 frittata ■ **PREP TIME** 15 minutes
COOK TIME 8 minutes ■ **STAND TIME** 3 minutes

4 ounces extra-lean, low-sodium ham slices, chopped

1 cup thinly sliced Vidalia onion

1 1/2 cups egg substitute

1/3 cup shredded, reduced-fat, sharp cheddar cheese

1 Place a medium nonstick skillet over medium-high heat until hot. Coat the skillet with nonstick cooking spray, add ham, and cook until beginning to lightly brown, about 2–3 minutes, stirring frequently. Remove from skillet and set aside on separate plate.

2 Reduce the heat to medium, coat the skillet with nonstick cooking spray, add onions, and cook 4 minutes or until beginning to turn golden, stirring frequently.

3 Reduce the heat to medium low, add ham to the onions, and cook 1 minute (this allows the flavors to blend and the skillet to cool slightly before the eggs are added). Pour egg substitute evenly over all, cover, and cook 8 minutes or until puffy and set.

4 Remove the skillet from the heat, sprinkle cheese evenly over all, cover, and let stand 3 minutes to melt the cheese and develop flavors.

EXCHANGES / CHOICES

1 Nonstarchy Vegetable
2 Protein, lean

Calories	110
Calories from Fat	20
Total Fat	2.0 g
Saturated Fat	1.1 g
Trans Fat	0.0 g
Cholesterol	20 mg
Sodium	460 mg
Potassium	250 mg
Total Carbohydrate	6 g
Dietary Fiber	0 g
Sugars	4 g
Protein	17 g
Phosphorus	125 mg

COOK'S TIP

If Vidalia onions are not available, use any other sweet variety, such as Texas Sweet.

Cheesy Mushroom Omelet

SERVES 2 ■ **SERVING SIZE** 1/2 omelet ■ **PREP TIME** 4 minutes ■ **COOK TIME** 6 minutes

6 ounces sliced mushrooms

1/8 teaspoon black pepper

1/3 cup finely chopped green onion
(green and white parts)

1 cup egg substitute

2 tablespoons crumbled bleu cheese
(about 1/4 cup) or 1/4 cup shredded,
reduced-fat, sharp cheddar cheese

1 Place a small skillet over medium-high heat until hot. Coat with nonstick cooking spray and add mushrooms and pepper. Coat the mushrooms with nonstick cooking spray and cook 4 minutes or until soft, stirring frequently.

2 Add the onions and cook 1 minute longer. Set the pan aside.

3 Place another small skillet over medium heat until hot. Coat with nonstick cooking spray and add the egg substitute. Cook 1 minute without stirring. Using a rubber spatula, lift up the edges to allow the uncooked portion to run under. Cook 1–2 minutes longer or until eggs are almost set and beginning to puff up slightly.

4 Spoon the mushroom mixture on one half of the omelet, sprinkle the cheese evenly over the mushrooms, and gently fold over. Cut in half to serve.

EXCHANGES / CHOICES

1 Nonstarchy Vegetable
2 Protein, lean

Calories	110
Calories from Fat	20
Total Fat	2.5 g
Saturated Fat	1.4 g
Trans Fat	0.1 g
Cholesterol	5 mg
Sodium	340 mg
Potassium	510 mg
Total Carbohydrate	6 g
Dietary Fiber	1 g
Sugars	3 g
Protein	16 g
Phosphorus	125 mg

COOK'S TIP

To double this recipe, cook all of the mushrooms and onions and set them aside. Then make 2 omelets, topping each with half of the mushroom mixture and the cheese. Serve 4 people each one omelet half.

Breakfast Grilled
Swiss Cheese and Rye

SERVES 2 ▪ **SERVING SIZE** 1 open-faced sandwich ▪ **PREP TIME** 4 minutes ▪ **COOK TIME** 7 minutes

2 slices rye bread

4 teaspoons reduced-fat margarine (35% vegetable oil)

2 large eggs

1 1/2 ounces sliced, reduced-fat Swiss cheese, torn in small pieces

1. Spread one side of each bread slice with 1 teaspoon margarine and set aside.

2. Place a medium skillet over medium heat until hot. Coat with nonstick cooking spray and add the egg substitute. Cook 1 minute without stirring. Using a rubber spatula, lift up the edges to allow the uncooked portion to run under. Cook 1–2 minutes longer or until eggs are almost set and beginning to puff up slightly. Flip and cook 30 seconds.

3. Remove the skillet from the heat and spoon half of the eggs on the unbuttered sides of two of the bread slices. Arrange equal amounts of the cheese evenly over each piece.

4. Return the skillet to medium heat until hot. Coat the skillet with nonstick cooking spray. Add the two sandwiches and cook 3 minutes. If the cheese doesn't melt when frying the sandwich bottom, put it under the broiler until brown. Using a serrated knife, cut each sandwich in half.

EXCHANGES / CHOICES

1 Starch
2 Protein, medium fat
1/2 Fat

Calories	250
Calories from Fat	120
Total Fat	13.0 g
Saturated Fat	4.4 g
Trans Fat	0.0 g
Cholesterol	200 mg
Sodium	360 mg
Potassium	150 mg
Total Carbohydrate	17 g
Dietary Fiber	2 g
Sugars	2 g
Protein	16 g
Phosphorus	265 mg

Sausage Potato Skillet Casserole

SERVES 4 ■ **SERVING SIZE** 1 cup ■ **PREP TIME** 10 minutes
COOK TIME 17 minutes ■ **STAND TIME** 5 minutes

5 ounces reduced-fat, smoked turkey sausage, kielbasa style

2 cups chopped onion

4 cups frozen hash brown potatoes with peppers and onions

1/3 cup shredded, reduced-fat, sharp cheddar cheese

1. Cut the sausage in fourths lengthwise. Cut each piece of sausage in 1/4-inch pieces.

2. Place a large nonstick skillet over medium-high heat until hot. Coat the skillet with nonstick cooking spray, add sausage, and cook 3 minutes or until the sausage begins to brown, stirring frequently. Set the sausage aside on a separate plate.

3. Recoat the skillet with nonstick cooking spray, add the onions, and cook 5 minutes or until the onions begin to brown, stirring frequently.

4. Reduce the heat to medium, add the frozen potatoes and sausage, and cook 9 minutes or until the potatoes are lightly browned, stirring occasionally.

5. Remove the skillet from the heat, top with cheese, cover, and let stand 5 minutes to melt the cheese and develop flavors.

EXCHANGES / CHOICES

1 1/2 Starch
1 Nonstarchy Vegetable
1 Protein, lean

Calories	190
Calories from Fat	45
Total Fat	5.0 g
Saturated Fat	2.0 g
Trans Fat	0.0 g
Cholesterol	25 mg
Sodium	450 mg
Potassium	450 mg
Total Carbohydrate	26 g
Dietary Fiber	4 g
Sugars	5 g
Protein	9 g
Phosphorus	190 mg

COOK'S TIP

The generous amount of onion adds extra moisture and texture as well as great flavor to this dish—without overpowering it!

Raisin French Toast with Apricot Spread

SERVES 4 ■ **SERVING SIZE** 2 pieces of toast plus 2 tablespoons spread
PREP TIME 8 minutes per batch ■ **COOK TIME** 6 minutes per batch

8 slices whole-wheat cinnamon
   raisin bread

3 tablespoons no-trans-fat margarine
   (35% vegetable oil)

1/4 cup apricot or any flavor all-fruit
   spread

1 cup egg substitute (divided use)

EXCHANGES / CHOICES

2 Starch
1/2 Fruit
1 Protein, lean
1/2 Fat

Calories	260
Calories from Fat	50
Total Fat	6.0 g
Saturated Fat	1.4 g
Trans Fat	0.0 g
Cholesterol	0 mg
Sodium	390 mg
Potassium	230 mg
Total Carbohydrate	37 g
Dietary Fiber	4 g
Sugars	17 g
Protein	12 g
Phosphorus	75 mg

1. Arrange 4 bread slices on the bottom of a 13 × 9-inch baking pan. Pour 1/2 cup egg substitute evenly over all and turn several times to coat. Let stand 2 minutes to absorb egg slightly.

2. Meanwhile, using a fork, stir the margarine and fruit spread together in a small bowl until well blended.

3. Place a large nonstick skillet over medium heat until hot. Liberally coat the skillet with nonstick cooking spray, add 4 bread slices (leaving any remaining egg mixture in the baking pan), and cook 3 minutes.

4. Turn and cook 3 minutes longer or until the bread is golden brown. For darker toast, turn the slices again and cook 1 minute more. Set aside on a serving platter and cover to keep warm.

5. While the first batch is cooking, place the remaining bread slices in the baking pan and pour the remaining egg substitute evenly over all. Turn several times to coat. Cook as directed.

6. Serve each piece of toast topped with 1 tablespoon of the margarine mixture.

COOK'S TIP

Be sure to use a fork when mixing the margarine and fruit spread together . . . this helps the fruit spread break down and blend evenly. The fork acts like a small whisk!

Double-Duty Banana Pancakes

SERVES 8 ▪ **SERVING SIZE** 1 pancake ▪ **PREP TIME** 7 minutes ▪ **COOK TIME** 6 minutes

2 ripe medium bananas, thinly sliced

1 cup buckwheat pancake mix

3/4 cup plus 2 tablespoons fat-free milk

4 tablespoons light pancake syrup

1 Mash one half of the banana slices and place in a medium bowl with the pancake mix and the milk. Stir until just blended.

2 Place a large nonstick skillet over medium heat until hot. (To test, sprinkle with a few drops of water. If the water drops "dance" or jump in the pan, it's hot enough.) Coat the skillet with nonstick cooking spray, add two scant 1/4 cup measures of batter, and cook the pancakes until puffed and dry around the edges, about 1 minute.

3 Flip the pancakes and cook until golden on the bottom. Place on a plate and cover to keep warm.

4 Recoat the skillet with nonstick cooking spray, add three scant 1/4 cup measures of batter, and cook as directed. Repeat with the remaining batter.

5 Place 2 pancakes on each of 4 dinner plates, top with equal amounts of banana slices, and drizzle evenly with the syrup. If you like, place the dinner plates in a warm oven and add the pancakes as they are cooked.

EXCHANGES / CHOICES

1 Starch
1/2 Fruit

Calories	100
Calories from Fat	5
Total Fat	**0.5 g**
Saturated Fat	0.1 g
Trans Fat	0.0 g
Cholesterol	0 mg
Sodium	140 mg
Potassium	200 mg
Total Carbohydrate	**23 g**
Dietary Fiber	2 g
Sugars	9 g
Protein	**3 g**
Phosphorus	175 mg

COOK'S TIP

The bananas in these pancakes add great flavor and fiber.

Peach Cranberry Quick Bread

SERVES 14 ■ **SERVING SIZE** 1 slice ■ **PREP TIME** 8 minutes
COOK TIME 45 minutes ■ **COOL TIME** 20 minutes

1 (15.6-ounce) box cranberry quick bread and muffin mix

1 cup water

1/2 cup egg substitute or 4 large egg whites

2 tablespoons canola oil

2 cups chopped frozen and thawed unsweetened peaches

1 Preheat the oven to 375°F.

2 Coat a nonstick 9 × 5-inch loaf pan with nonstick cooking spray.

3 Beat the bread mix, water, egg substitute, and oil in a medium bowl for 50 strokes or until well blended. Stir in the peaches and spoon into the loaf pan. Bake 45 minutes or until a wooden toothpick comes out clean.

4 Place the loaf pan on a wire rack for 20 minutes before removing the bread from the pan. Cool completely for peak flavor and texture.

EXCHANGES / CHOICES

2 Carbohydrate
1/2 Fat

Calories	150
Calories from Fat	25
Total Fat	3.0 g
Saturated Fat	0.5 g
Trans Fat	0.1 g
Cholesterol	0 mg
Sodium	150 mg
Potassium	75 mg
Total Carbohydrate	29 g
Dietary Fiber	1 g
Sugars	15 g
Protein	3 g
Phosphorus	75 mg

COOK'S TIP

The peaches make this quick bread especially flavorful and moist. It freezes well, too!

SNACKS

Lime'd Blueberries

SERVES 6 ■ **SERVING SIZE** 1/3 cup ■ **PREP TIME** 5 minutes

2 cups frozen unsweetened blueberries, partially thawed

1/4 cup frozen grape juice concentrate

1 1/2 tablespoons lime juice

1 Place all ingredients in a medium bowl and toss gently.

2 Serve immediately for peak flavor and texture.

EXCHANGES / CHOICES
1 Fruit

Calories	50
Calories from Fat	5
Total Fat	0.5 g
Saturated Fat	0.0 g
Trans Fat	0.0 g
Cholesterol	0 mg
Sodium	5 mg
Potassium	50 mg
Total Carbohydrate	13 g
Dietary Fiber	1 g
Sugars	11 g
Protein	0 g
Phosphorus	10 mg

COOK'S TIP
To thaw the blueberries quickly, place them in a colander and run under cold water for 20 seconds. Shake off excess liquid.

Zesty Lemony Shrimp

SERVES 8 ■ **SERVING SIZE** 1/4 cup ■ **PREP TIME** 5 minutes ■ **COOK TIME** 7–10 minutes

12 ounces peeled raw medium shrimp, fresh, or frozen and thawed

2 tablespoons Worcestershire sauce

1 teaspoon lemon zest

3 tablespoons lemon juice

2 tablespoons no-trans-fat margarine (35% vegetable oil)

1 tablespoon finely chopped fresh parsley (optional)

1 Place a large nonstick skillet over medium heat until hot. Add the shrimp, Worcestershire sauce, lemon zest, and lemon juice to the skillet. Cook 5 minutes or until shrimp is opaque in center, stirring frequently.

2 Using a slotted spoon, remove the shrimp and set aside in serving bowl. Increase the heat to medium high, add the margarine, bring to a boil, and continue to boil 2 minutes or until the liquid measures 1/4 cup, stirring constantly.

3 Pour the sauce over the shrimp and sprinkle with 1 tablespoon finely chopped parsley, if desired. Serve with wooden toothpicks.

EXCHANGES / CHOICES
1 Protein, lean

Calories	50
Calories from Fat	5
Total Fat	0.5 g
Saturated Fat	0.2 g
Trans Fat	0.0 g
Cholesterol	70 mg
Sodium	95 mg
Potassium	140 mg
Total Carbohydrate	1 g
Dietary Fiber	0 g
Sugars	1 g
Protein	9 g
Phosphorus	90 mg

COOK'S TIP

Whenever a recipe calls for citrus zest, such as lemon, lime, or orange, wrap the unused fruit in plastic wrap and refrigerate for a later use. You're sure to need fresh citrus juice for the next recipe!

Creamy Apricot Fruit Dip

SERVES 4 ■ **SERVING SIZE** 2 tablespoons ■ **PREP TIME** 5 minutes

1/3 cup fat-free vanilla-flavored yogurt

1/4 cup fat-free whipped topping

2 tablespoons apricot all-fruit spread

2 cups whole strawberries or 2 medium
    apples, halved, cored, and sliced

1 In a small bowl, whisk the yogurt, whipped topping,
    and fruit spread until well blended.

2 Serve with fruit.

EXCHANGES / CHOICES
1 Fruit

Calories	60
Calories from Fat	0
Total Fat	0.0 g
Saturated Fat	0.0 g
Trans Fat	0.0 g
Cholesterol	0 mg
Sodium	15 mg
Potassium	150 mg
Total Carbohydrate	14 g
Dietary Fiber	2 g
Sugars	9 g
Protein	1 g
Phosphorus	40 mg

COOK'S TIP
Squeeze a small amount of orange juice over sliced apples
to prevent browning.

Bleu Cheese'd Pears

SERVES 4 ■ **SERVING SIZE** 5 pear slices with about 3/4 teaspoon cheese ■ **PREP TIME** 5 minutes

2 ounces fat-free cream cheese

3 1/2 tablespoons crumbled bleu cheese

2 medium firm pears, halved, cored, and sliced into 20 slices

1 In a small bowl, microwave the cheeses on HIGH for 10 seconds to soften. Use a rubber spatula to blend well.

2 Top each pear slice with 3/4 teaspoon cheese.

3 To prevent the pear slices from discoloring, toss them with a tablespoon of orange, pineapple, or lemon juice. Shake off the excess liquid before topping them with cheese.

EXCHANGES / CHOICES

1 Fruit
1/2 Fat

Calories	90
Calories from Fat	20
Total Fat	2.0 g
Saturated Fat	1.4 g
Trans Fat	0.1 g
Cholesterol	10 mg
Sodium	190 mg
Potassium	150 mg
Total Carbohydrate	14 g
Dietary Fiber	3 g
Sugars	9 g
Protein	4 g
Phosphorus	115 mg

COOK'S TIP

To make pretty hors d'oeuvres, use a small pastry bag to top each pear with cheese. Be sure to toss the pear slices with juice first to prevent discoloration.

Basil Spread and Water Crackers

SERVES 4 ■ **SERVING SIZE** 1 tablespoon spread plus 3 crackers ■ **PREP TIME** 5 minutes

2 ounces reduced-fat garlic and herb cream cheese

1/2 cup finely chopped fresh basil

12 fat-free water crackers

1 Stir the cream cheese and basil together in a small bowl until well blended.

2 Place 1 teaspoon spread on each cracker.

EXCHANGES / CHOICES

1/2 Starch
1/2 Fat

Calories	70
Calories from Fat	20
Total Fat	2.0 g
Saturated Fat	1.0 g
Trans Fat	0.0 g
Cholesterol	0 mg
Sodium	200 mg
Potassium	45 mg
Total Carbohydrate	9 g
Dietary Fiber	0 g
Sugars	1 g
Protein	3 g
Phosphorus	100 mg

COOK'S TIP

You can stir in a small amount of milk to this cream cheese and make a delicious dip for fresh vegetables.

Pork and Avocado Salad

page 57

Baby Carrots and Spicy Cream Dip

SERVES 4 ■ **SERVING SIZE** 2 tablespoons dip plus 12 baby carrots
PREP TIME 5 minutes ■ **STAND TIME** 10 minutes

1/3 cup fat-free sour cream

3 tablespoons reduced-fat tub-style
   cream cheese

3/4 teaspoon hot pepper sauce

1/8 teaspoon salt

48 baby carrots

1 Stir the sour cream, cream cheese, pepper sauce, and salt together until well blended.

2 Let stand at least 10 minutes to develop flavors and mellow slightly. Serve with carrots.

EXCHANGES / CHOICES

1/2 Carbohydrate
2 Nonstarchy Vegetable

Calories	90
Calories from Fat	20
Total Fat	2.5 g
Saturated Fat	1.4 g
Trans Fat	0.0 g
Cholesterol	10 mg
Sodium	240 mg
Potassium	430 mg
Total Carbohydrate	16 g
Dietary Fiber	3 g
Sugars	7 g
Protein	3 g
Phosphorus	80 mg

COOK'S TIP

You can cover this dip with plastic wrap and refrigerate it up to 1 week.

Crostini with Kalamata Tomato

SERVES 4 ■ **SERVING SIZE** 3 slices crostini ■ **PREP TIME** 10 minutes
COOK TIME 10 minutes ■ **STAND TIME** 10 minutes

4 ounces multigrain baguette bread, cut in 12 slices (about 1/4 inch thick)

1 small tomato, finely chopped

9 small kalamata olives, pitted and finely chopped

2 tablespoons chopped fresh basil

1 Preheat the oven to 350°F.

2 Arrange the bread slices on a baking sheet and bake 10 minutes or until just golden on the edges. Remove from the heat and cool completely.

3 Meanwhile, stir the remaining ingredients together in a small bowl. Spread 1 tablespoon of the mixture on each bread slice.

EXCHANGES / CHOICES
1 Starch

Calories	90
Calories from Fat	20
Total Fat	2.0 g
Saturated Fat	0.3 g
Trans Fat	0.0 g
Cholesterol	0 mg
Sodium	220 mg
Potassium	90 mg
Total Carbohydrate	16 g
Dietary Fiber	1 g
Sugars	2 g
Protein	3 g
Phosphorus	70 mg

COOK'S TIP
For a thicker topping, drain the tomato mixture before spreading it on the bread.

Asian Marinated Mushrooms

SERVES 4 ■ **SERVING SIZE** 4 mushrooms ■ **PREP TIME** 5 minutes
MARINATE TIME 30 minutes ■ **COOK TIME** 8 minutes

8 ounces whole medium mushrooms, stemmed and wiped clean with damp paper towel

1/4 tablespoons lite soy sauce

2 tablespoons lime juice

1 teaspoon extra virgin olive oil

1. Place the mushrooms, soy sauce, lime juice, and oil in a large plastic zippered bag. Seal the bag and shake to coat completely. Let stand 30 minutes. Meanwhile, preheat the broiler.

2. Place mushroom mixture (with marinade) in an 8-inch pie pan or baking pan and broil 4 inches away from heat source for 8 minutes or until the mushrooms begin to brown, stirring frequently.

3. Serve with wooden toothpicks and marinade. Top with 2 tablespoons chopped fresh parsley, if desired.

EXCHANGES / CHOICES
1 Nonstarchy Vegetable

Calories	30
Calories from Fat	15
Total Fat	1.5 g
Saturated Fat	0.2 g
Trans Fat	0.0 g
Cholesterol	0 mg
Sodium	240 mg
Potassium	190 mg
Total Carbohydrate	3 g
Dietary Fiber	1 g
Sugars	1 g
Protein	2 g
Phosphorus	55 mg

COOK'S TIP
This appetizer is delicious served hot or at room temperature.

Tomato Cilantro Salsa

SERVES 4 ■ **SERVING SIZE** 1/4 cup salsa plus 3/4 ounce chips ■ **PREP TIME** 10 minutes

3 medium tomatoes, seeded and finely chopped

1/4 cup chopped cilantro

2 medium jalapeño peppers, stems removed, halved, seeded, and minced

3–4 tablespoons lime juice

1/8 teaspoon salt

3 ounces baked low-fat tortilla chips

1 Combine all ingredients except chips in a small bowl. Serve with chips.

2 For peak flavor, serve this within 1 hour of preparing it.

EXCHANGES / CHOICES
1 Starch
1 Nonstarchy Vegetable

Calories	110
Calories from Fat	10
Total Fat	1.0 g
Saturated Fat	0.2 g
Trans Fat	0.0 g
Cholesterol	0 mg
Sodium	230 mg
Potassium	390 mg
Total Carbohydrate	25 g
Dietary Fiber	3 g
Sugars	4 g
Protein	4 g
Phosphorus	105 mg

COOK'S TIP

It's important to seed the tomato before chopping it—otherwise the salsa is too watery. For a milder salsa, use 1 tablespoon minced green bell pepper and 2–3 drops hot pepper sauce. Be sure to remove the seeds and membrane from the jalapeño pepper, or your salsa will be extra hot!

Sweet Peanut Buttery Dip

SERVES 4 ■ **SERVING SIZE** 1/2 banana plus 2 tablespoons dip ■ **PREP TIME** 5 minutes

1/3 cup fat-free vanilla-flavored yogurt

2 tablespoons reduced-fat peanut butter

2 teaspoons packed dark brown sugar

2 medium bananas, sliced

1 Using a fork or whisk, stir the yogurt, peanut butter, and brown sugar together in a small bowl until completely blended.

2 Serve with banana slices and wooden toothpicks, if desired.

EXCHANGES / CHOICES

1 Fruit
1/2 Carbohydrate
1/2 Fat

Calories	120
Calories from Fat	25
Total Fat	3.0 g
Saturated Fat	0.6 g
Trans Fat	0.0 g
Cholesterol	0 mg
Sodium	40 mg
Potassium	310 mg
Total Carbohydrate	21 g
Dietary Fiber	2 g
Sugars	12 g
Protein	3 g
Phosphorus	65 mg

COOK'S TIP

This recipe is also delicious with honey instead of brown sugar. You can cover and refrigerate this dip for up to 5 days.

Dilled Chex Toss

SERVES 18 ■ **SERVING SIZE** 1/3 cup ■ **PREP TIME** 5 minutes ■ **COOK TIME** 30 minutes

6 cups multi-grain or Wheat Chex cereal

4-ounce packet ranch salad dressing mix

1 tablespoon dried dill

2 tablespoons extra virgin olive oil

1 Preheat the oven to 175°F.

2 Place the cereal, dressing mix, and dill in a large zippered plastic bag. Seal and shake gently to blend well.

3 Place the mixture on a large rimmed baking sheet or jelly roll pan, drizzle the oil evenly over all, and stir thoroughly to blend. Spread out in a single layer and bake 30 minutes or until browned lightly, stirring once.

EXCHANGES / CHOICES
1/2 Starch
1/2 Fat

Calories	50
Calories from Fat	15
Total Fat	1.5 g
Saturated Fat	0.2 g
Trans Fat	0.0 g
Cholesterol	0 mg
Sodium	200 mg
Potassium	30 mg
Total Carbohydrate	8 g
Dietary Fiber	1 g
Sugars	1 g
Protein	1 g
Phosphorus	20 mg

COOK'S TIP
Store this tasty toss in an airtight container in a cool, dry area up to 2 weeks.

Tuna Salad Stuffed Eggs

SERVES 4 ■ SERVING SIZE 2 egg halves ■ PREP TIME 5 minutes
COOK TIME 10 minutes ■ STAND TIME 1 minute

4 large eggs

1 (2.6-ounce) packet tuna (or 5-ounce can of tuna packed in water, rinsed and well drained)

2 tablespoons reduced-fat mayonnaise

1 1/2–2 tablespoons sweet pickle relish

1 Place eggs in a medium saucepan and cover with cold water. Bring to a boil over high heat, then reduce the heat and simmer 10 minutes.

2 Meanwhile, stir the tuna, mayonnaise, and relish together in a small bowl.

3 When the eggs are cooked, remove them from the water and let stand one minute before peeling under cold running water. Cut eggs in half, lengthwise, and discard 4 egg yolk halves and place the other 2 egg yolk halves in the tuna mixture and stir with a rubber spatula until well blended. Spoon equal amounts of the tuna mixture in each of the egg halves.

4 Serve immediately, or cover with plastic wrap and refrigerate up to 24 hours.

EXCHANGES / CHOICES

1 Protein, lean
1 Fat

Calories	90
Calories from Fat	40
Total Fat	4.5 g
Saturated Fat	1.1 g
Trans Fat	0.0 g
Cholesterol	105 mg
Sodium	240 mg
Potassium	105 mg
Total Carbohydrate	3 g
Dietary Fiber	0 g
Sugars	2 g
Protein	9 g
Phosphorus	85 mg

SALADS

Minted Carrot Salad

SERVES 4 ■ SERVING SIZE 3/4 cup salad ■ PREP TIME 10 minutes
COOK TIME 1 minute ■ CHILL TIME 1 hour

3 cups thinly sliced carrots (about
    12 ounces total)

1 tablespoon extra-virgin olive oil

1 tablespoon cider vinegar

1/3 cup chopped fresh mint (or basil)

1   Bring 4 cups water to a rolling boil in a large saucepan.
Add the carrots, return to a rolling boil, and cook
30 seconds. Immediately drain in a colander and run
under cold water to cool completely. Drain well.

2   Place carrots in a shallow bowl. Top with remaining
ingredients and sprinkle evenly with 1/4 teaspoon
salt and 1/4 teaspoon pepper. Serve immediately
or cover and refrigerate up to 1 hour before serving.

EXCHANGES / CHOICES

1 1/2 Nonstarchy Vegetable
1 Fat

Calories	75
Calories from Fat	40
Total Fat	4 g
Saturated Fat	0.5 g
Trans Fat	0 g
Cholesterol	0 mg
Sodium	70 mg
Potassium	360 mg
Total Carbohydrate	10 g
Dietary Fiber	4 g
Sugars	5 g
Protein	1 g
Phosphorus	40 mg

Carrot Cranberry Matchstick Salad

SERVES 4 ■ **SERVING SIZE** 3/4 cup salad ■ **PREP TIME** 5 minutes ■ **CHILL TIME** 1 hour

3 cups matchstick carrots

1 poblano chili pepper, chopped

1/3 cup dried cranberries

Zest and juice of 1 medium lemon

1 Combine the ingredients with 1/8 teaspoon salt in a large bowl. Cover and refrigerate 1 hour before serving.

EXCHANGES / CHOICES

2 Vegetable
1/2 Other carbohydrate

Calories	70
Calories from Fat	0
Total Fat	0 g
Saturated Fat	0 g
Trans Fat	0.0 g
Cholesterol	0 mg
Sodium	105 mg
Potassium	335 mg
Total Carbohydrate	19 g
Dietary Fiber	4 g
Sugars	11 g
Protein	1 g
Phosphorus	40 mg

Broccoli Almond Slaw

SERVES 4 ■ **SERVING SIZE** 3/4 cup ■ **PREP TIME** 5 minutes
COOK TIME 2 minutes ■ **CHILL TIME** 1 hour

2 ounces slivered almonds

4 cups broccoli slaw

2 tablespoons sugar

3 tablespoons white balsamic vinegar

1 Heat a skillet over medium-high heat. Add the almonds and cook 2 minutes or until beginning to lightly brown, stirring frequently.

2 Combine the almonds and 1/4 teaspoon salt and 1/4 teaspoon pepper, if desired, with the remaining ingredients in a large bowl. Cover and refrigerate 1 hour before serving.

EXCHANGES / CHOICES
2 Vegetable
1/2 Other carbohydrate
1 1/2 Fat

Calories	150
Calories from Fat	60
Total Fat	7 g
Saturated Fat	0.6 g
Trans Fat	0.0 g
Cholesterol	0 mg
Sodium	120 mg
Potassium	390 mg
Total Carbohydrate	17 g
Dietary Fiber	4 g
Sugars	10 g
Protein	6 g
Phosphorus	130 mg

COOK'S TIP
May replace almonds with shelled pistachios, if desired.

Chicken Kale Salad
with Fresh Ginger Dressing

SERVES 4 ■ **SERVING SIZE** 2 cups salad; 3 ounces cooked chicken; and 3 tablespoons dressing
PREP TIME 5 minutes ■ **COOK TIME** 12 minutes

1 pound boneless, skinless
  chicken breast

8 cups packed spinach with baby
  kale greens

3/4 cup light raspberry salad dressing,
  such as Newman's Own

2 to 3 teaspoons grated gingerroot

1 Heat a grill or grill pan over medium-high heat.
   Coat the chicken with cooking spray, sprinkle with
   1/4 teaspoon salt and 1/4 teaspoon pepper, if desired.
   Cook 6 minutes on each side or until no longer
   pink in center. Let cool and thinly slice.

2 Place equal amounts of the greens and chicken on
   four dinner plates. Whisk together the salad dressing
   and ginger until well blended. Spoon equal amounts
   over all.

EXCHANGES / CHOICES
1 Vegetable
3 1/2 Protein, lean
1 Fat

Calories	230
Calories from Fat	90
Total Fat	10 g
Saturated Fat	1.3 g
Trans Fat	0.0 g
Cholesterol	85 mg
Sodium	440 mg
Potassium	760 mg
Total Carbohydrate	6 g
Dietary Fiber	2 g
Sugars	3 g
Protein	28 g
Phosphorus	285 mg

Pork and Avocado Salad

SERVES 4 ■ **SERVING SIZE** about 1 1/3 cups ■ **PREP TIME** 5 minutes ■ **COOK TIME** 10 minutes

1 pound boneless center-cut pork
   loin chops

2 ripe medium avocados, chopped

1/4 cup fresh lemon

1 cup chopped fresh parsley or cilantro

1 Heat a grill pan or large skillet coated with cooking spray over medium-high heat. Cook the pork 4 minutes on each side or until slightly pink in center. Place on cutting board to cool.

2 Chop pork and place in a large bowl with 1/2 teaspoon salt and 1/2 teaspoon pepper, if desired, and remaining ingredients; toss gently until well blended.

EXCHANGES / CHOICES

1 Nonstarchy Vegetable
3 1/2 Protein, lean
2 Fat

Calories	260
Calories from Fat	120
Total Fat	13 g
Saturated Fat	2.5 g
Trans Fat	0.0 g
Cholesterol	70 mg
Sodium	85 mg
Potassium	830 mg
Total Carbohydrate	8 g
Dietary Fiber	5 g
Sugars	1 g
Protein	28 g
Phosphorus	330 mg

COOK'S TIP

For a variation, spoon equal amounts in 12 leaves of romaine and serve as a lettuce wrap.

COOK'S TIP

May use boneless, skinless chicken breast instead of pork, if desired.

Lemony Asparagus Spear Salad

SERVES 4 ■ **SERVING SIZE** 5 spears ■ **PREP TIME** 6 minutes ■ **COOK TIME** 1 minute

1 pound asparagus spears, trimmed

1 tablespoon basil pesto sauce

2 teaspoons lemon juice

1/4 teaspoon salt

1 Cover asparagus with water in a large skillet and bring to a boil, then cover tightly and cook 1 minute or until tender-crisp.

2 Immediately drain the asparagus in a colander and run under cold water to cool. Place the asparagus on paper towels to drain, then place on a serving platter.

3 Top the asparagus with the pesto and roll the spears back and forth to coat completely. Drizzle with lemon juice and sprinkle with salt. Flavors are at their peak if you serve this within 30 minutes.

EXCHANGES / CHOICES

1 Nonstarchy Vegetable

Calories	25
Calories from Fat	10
Total Fat	1.0 g
Saturated Fat	0.2 g
Trans Fat	0.0 g
Cholesterol	0 mg
Sodium	190 mg
Potassium	125 mg
Total Carbohydrate	3 g
Dietary Fiber	1 g
Sugars	1 g
Protein	2 g
Phosphorus	30 mg

COOK'S TIP

You can cook the asparagus ahead of time and refrigerate it, but wait until serving time to add the remaining ingredients.

Artichoke Tomato Toss

SERVES 4 ■ **SERVING SIZE** 1/2 cup ■ **PREP TIME** 4 minutes

1/2 of a 14-ounce can quartered artichoke hearts, drained

1 cup grape tomatoes, halved

1 tablespoons fat-free Caesar or Italian dressing

1 ounce crumbled, reduced-fat, sun-dried tomato and basil feta cheese

2 tablespoons chopped fresh parsley (optional)

1. In a medium bowl, toss the artichoke hearts, tomatoes, and dressing gently, yet thoroughly. Add the feta and toss gently again.

2. Serve immediately or cover with plastic wrap and refrigerate up to 3 days.

EXCHANGES / CHOICES
1 Nonstarchy Vegetable
1/2 Fat

Calories	45
Calories from Fat	15
Total Fat	1.5 g
Saturated Fat	0.9 g
Trans Fat	0.0 g
Cholesterol	5 mg
Sodium	270 mg
Potassium	180 mg
Total Carbohydrate	6 g
Dietary Fiber	3 g
Sugars	2 g
Protein	3 g
Phosphorus	55 mg

COOK'S TIP
Toss very lightly after adding the feta for peak color and texture.

Creamy Dill Cucumbers

SERVES 4 ▪ **SERVING SIZE** 1/2 cup ▪ **PREP TIME** 6 minutes

1/4 cup plain fat-free yogurt

1 tablespoon reduced-fat mayonnaise

1/2 teaspoon dried dill

1/4 teaspoon salt

2 cups peeled diced cucumber

1 Stir the yogurt, mayonnaise, dill, and salt together in a small bowl until completely blended.

2 Place the cucumbers in a medium bowl, add the yogurt mixture, and toss gently to coat completely.

3 Serve within 30 minutes for peak flavors and texture.

EXCHANGES / CHOICES
1 Nonstarchy Vegetable

Calories	25
Calories from Fat	10
Total Fat	1.0 g
Saturated Fat	0.2 g
Trans Fat	0.0 g
Cholesterol	0 mg
Sodium	190 mg
Potassium	130 mg
Total Carbohydrate	3 g
Dietary Fiber	0 g
Sugars	2 g
Protein	1 g
Phosphorus	40 mg

COOK'S TIP
For variety, try using fat-free sour cream instead of the yogurt.

Bacon Onion Potato Salad

SERVES 4 ■ **SERVING SIZE** 1/2 cup ■ **PREP TIME** 10 minutes
COOK TIME 4 minutes ■ **CHILL TIME** 2 hours (optional)

12 ounces unpeeled red potatoes, diced (about 3 cups)

3 tablespoons reduced-fat ranch salad dressing

1/2 cup finely chopped green onion

2 tablespoons real bacon bits (not imitation)

1 Bring water to boil in a medium saucepan over high heat. Add the potatoes and return to a boil. Reduce the heat, cover tightly, and cook 4 minutes or until just tender when pierced with a fork.

2 Drain the potatoes in a colander and run under cold water until cool, about 30 seconds. Drain well and place in a medium bowl with the remaining ingredients. Toss gently to blend well.

3 Serve immediately or cover with plastic wrap and refrigerate 2 hours for a more blended flavor. To serve, add salt, if desired and toss.

EXCHANGES / CHOICES

1 Starch
1/2 Fat

Calories	110
Calories from Fat	30
Total Fat	3.5 g
Saturated Fat	0.9 g
Trans Fat	0.0 g
Cholesterol	5 mg
Sodium	250 mg
Potassium	490 mg
Total Carbohydrate	16 g
Dietary Fiber	2 g
Sugars	2 g
Protein	4 g
Phosphorus	80 mg

COOK'S TIP

For peak flavor and texture, serve this salad the same day you make it.

Balsamic Bean Salsa Salad

SERVES 4 ■ **SERVING SIZE** 1/2 cup ■ **PREP TIME** 6 minutes ■ **STAND TIME** 15 minutes

15-ounce can black beans, rinsed and drained

1/2 cup chopped red bell pepper

1/4 cup finely chopped red onion

2 tablespoons balsamic vinegar

1 Toss all ingredients in a medium bowl.

2 Let stand 15 minutes to develop flavors.

EXCHANGES / CHOICES

1 Starch
1 Protein, lean

Calories	100
Calories from Fat	5
Total Fat	0.5 g
Saturated Fat	0.1 g
Trans Fat	0.0 g
Cholesterol	0 mg
Sodium	80 mg
Potassium	280 mg
Total Carbohydrate	18 g
Dietary Fiber	6 g
Sugars	4 g
Protein	6 g
Phosphorus	95 mg

COOK'S TIP

You can cover this salad with plastic wrap and refrigerate up to 8 hours.

Tangy Sweet Carrot Pepper Salad

SERVES 4 ■ **SERVING SIZE** 1/2 cup ■ **PREP TIME** 12 minutes
COOK TIME 1 minute ■ **STAND TIME** 30 minutes (optional)

1 1/2 cups peeled sliced carrots
(about 1/8-inch thick)

2 tablespoons water

3/4 cup thinly sliced green bell pepper

1/3 cup thinly sliced onion

1/4 cup reduced-fat Catalina dressing

1. Place carrots and water in a shallow, microwave-safe dish, such as a glass pie plate. Cover with plastic wrap and microwave on HIGH for 1 minute or until carrots are just tender-crisp. Be careful not to overcook them—the carrots should retain some crispness.

2. Immediately place the carrots in a colander and run under cold water about 30 seconds to cool. Shake to drain and place the carrots on paper towels to dry further. Dry the dish.

3. When the carrots are completely cool, return them to the dish, add the remaining ingredients, and toss gently to coat.

4. Serve immediately, or chill 30 minutes for a more blended flavor. Flavors are at their peak if you serve this salad within 30 minutes of adding dressing.

EXCHANGES / CHOICES

1/2 Carbohydrate
1 Nonstarchy Vegetable

Calories	60
Calories from Fat	5
Total Fat	0.5 g
Saturated Fat	0.1 g
Trans Fat	0.0 g
Cholesterol	0 mg
Sodium	200 mg
Potassium	210 mg
Total Carbohydrate	11 g
Dietary Fiber	2 g
Sugars	7 g
Protein	1 g
Phosphorus	25 mg

COOK'S TIP

To make this salad ahead of time, combine the prepared carrots with the peppers and onions up to 24 hours in advance. Toss with the dressing 30 minutes before serving.

Crispy Crunch Coleslaw

SERVES 4 ■ **SERVING SIZE** 1/2 cup ■ **PREP TIME** 7 minutes ■ **CHILL TIME** 3 hours

3 cups shredded cabbage mix with carrots and red cabbage

1 medium green bell pepper, finely chopped

2–3 tablespoons apple cider vinegar

2 tablespoons Splenda

1/8 teaspoon salt

1 Place all ingredients in a large zippered plastic bag, seal tightly, and shake to blend thoroughly.

2 Refrigerate 3 hours before serving to blend flavors. This salad tastes best served the same day you make it.

EXCHANGES / CHOICES

1 Nonstarchy Vegetable

Calories	20
Calories from Fat	0
Total Fat	0.0 g
Saturated Fat	0.0 g
Trans Fat	0.0 g
Cholesterol	0 mg
Sodium	85 mg
Potassium	170 mg
Total Carbohydrate	4 g
Dietary Fiber	2 g
Sugars	2 g
Protein	0 g
Phosphorus	20 mg

COOK'S TIP

For more heat, use a poblano chili pepper in place of the green bell pepper.

Thousand Isle Wedges

SERVES 4 ■ **SERVING SIZE** 1 wedge plus 2 tablespoons dressing ■ **PREP TIME** 5 minutes

3 tablespoons no-salt ketchup

1/8 teaspoon salt

1 tablespoon reduced-fat mayonnaise

1/3 cup fat-free buttermilk

1/2 small head iceberg lettuce,
  cut in 4 wedges

1 Stir the ketchup, salt, and mayonnaise together in a small bowl until smooth. Add the buttermilk and blend thoroughly.

2 Place a lettuce wedge on each salad plate, spoon 2 tablespoons dressing on top of each wedge, and sprinkle evenly with black pepper, if desired.

EXCHANGES / CHOICES

1/2 Carbohydrate

Calories	40
Calories from Fat	10
Total Fat	1.0 g
Saturated Fat	0.1 g
Trans Fat	0.0 g
Cholesterol	0 mg
Sodium	125 mg
Potassium	140 mg
Total Carbohydrate	6 g
Dietary Fiber	1 g
Sugars	5 g
Protein	1 g
Phosphorus	30 mg

COOK'S TIP

Be sure to combine the ingredients as directed before adding the buttermilk—otherwise it's difficult to remove the lumps! You won't believe how much better this Thousand Island dressing tastes than the store-bought versions.

Mild Mustard Romaine Salad

SERVES 4 ■ **SERVING SIZE** 2 cups salad plus 2 tablespoons dressing ■ **PREP TIME** 5 minutes

1/2 cup fat-free sour cream

2 tablespoons water

2 teaspoons prepared mustard

2 teaspoons reduced-fat mayonnaise

1/4 teaspoon salt

8 cups packed torn Romaine lettuce

Coarsely ground black pepper to taste
(optional)

1 Stir the sour cream, water, mustard, mayonnaise, and salt together in a small bowl until well blended.

2 Place the lettuce in a large bowl, add the dressing, and toss gently to coat. Sprinkle with black pepper, if desired.

EXCHANGES / CHOICES
1/2 Carbohydrate

Calories	50
Calories from Fat	10
Total Fat	1.0 g
Saturated Fat	0.3 g
Trans Fat	0.0 g
Cholesterol	5 mg
Sodium	230 mg
Potassium	260 mg
Total Carbohydrate	8 g
Dietary Fiber	2 g
Sugars	2 g
Protein	2 g
Phosphorus	60 mg

COOK'S TIP
For peak flavor, be sure to toss this salad thoroughly to evenly coat the lettuce.

Chicken Kale Salad with
Fresh Ginger Dressing
page 56

Cumin'd Salsa Salad

SERVES 4 ■ **SERVING SIZE** 2 cups ■ **PREP TIME** 3 minutes

3/4 cup mild or medium salsa fresca
(pico de gallo)

2 tablespoons water

1/4 teaspoon ground cumin

8 cups shredded lettuce

20 baked bite-sized multi-grain tortilla
chips, coarsely crumbled (1 ounce)

1 Stir the salsa, water, and cumin together in a small
bowl.

2 Place 2 cups of lettuce on each of 4 salad plates,
spoon 3 tablespoons picante mixture over each salad,
and top with chips.

EXCHANGES / CHOICES

1/2 Starch
1 Nonstarchy Vegetable

Calories	60
Calories from Fat	20
Total Fat	2.0 g
Saturated Fat	0.3 g
Trans Fat	0.0 g
Cholesterol	0 mg
Sodium	40 mg
Potassium	240 mg
Total Carbohydrate	9 g
Dietary Fiber	2 g
Sugars	3 g
Protein	2 g
Phosphorus	35 mg

COOK'S TIP

For variation, add 1 cup diced cucumber or matchstick carrots to the shredded lettuce.

Pear and Bleu Cheese Greens

SERVES 4 ■ **SERVING SIZE** 2 cups ■ **PREP TIME** 4 minutes

6 cups spring greens

1 1/3 cups firm pear slices or green apple slices

6 tablespoons fat-free raspberry vinaigrette

3 tablespoons crumbled reduced-fat bleu cheese

1 Place 1 1/2 cups of the greens on each of 4 salad plates. Arrange 1/3 cup pear slices on each serving.

2 Top with 1 1/2 tablespoons dressing and 3/4 tablespoon of the cheese. Serve immediately.

EXCHANGES / CHOICES

1/2 Fruit
1/2 Carbohydrate

Calories	80
Calories from Fat	10
Total Fat	1.0 g
Saturated Fat	0.7 g
Trans Fat	0.0 g
Cholesterol	5 mg
Sodium	230 mg
Potassium	190 mg
Total Carbohydrate	15 g
Dietary Fiber	2 g
Sugars	11 g
Protein	2 g
Phosphorus	40 mg

COOK'S TIP

This recipe is also delicious made with fresh berries and goat cheese (cut in small pieces).

Caesar'd Chicken Salad

SERVES 4 ■ **SERVING SIZE** 1/2 cup ■ **PREP TIME** 5 minutes ■ **CHILL TIME** 2 hours

1/4 cup fat-free mayonnaise

3 tablespoons fat-free Caesar salad dressing

2 1/2 cups cooked diced chicken breast

1/2 cup finely chopped green onion (green and white parts)

1 Stir the mayonnaise and salad dressing together in a medium bowl. Add the chicken, onions, and black pepper, if desired, and stir until well coated.

2 Cover with plastic wrap and refrigerate at least 2 hours to allow flavors to blend. You may refrigerate this salad up to 24 hours before serving.

EXCHANGES / CHOICES
4 Protein, lean

Calories	170
Calories from Fat	30
Total Fat	3.5 g
Saturated Fat	1.0 g
Trans Fat	0.0 g
Cholesterol	75 mg
Sodium	460 mg
Potassium	270 mg
Total Carbohydrate	4 g
Dietary Fiber	1 g
Sugars	2 g
Protein	28 g
Phosphorus	210 mg

COOK'S TIP
No leftover chicken? Cook 1 pound chicken breast meat in the microwave. Place the chicken on a microwave-safe plate, cover with plastic wrap, and cook on HIGH 2 minutes. Turn and cook 1–2 minutes longer or until the chicken is barely pink in the center. Remove and let stand 15 minutes to cool completely, then cut into bite-sized pieces.

Feta'd Tuna with Greens

SERVES 4 ■ **SERVING SIZE** 1 1/2 cups ■ **PREP TIME** 6 minutes

6 cups torn Boston Bibb lettuce, red leaf lettuce, or spring greens

3 tablespoons fat-free Caesar salad dressing

2 ounces crumbled, reduced-fat, sun-dried tomato and basil feta cheese

1 (6.4-ounce) packet tuna, broken in large chunks

1 Place the lettuce and salad dressing in a large bowl and toss gently, yet thoroughly, to coat completely.

2 Place 1 1/2 cups of lettuce on each of 4 salad plates. Sprinkle each salad with 1 tablespoon feta and lightly flake equal amounts of tuna in the center of each serving. If desired, add a small amount of dressing (such as fat-free Caesar) to the lettuce.

EXCHANGES / CHOICES

2 Protein, lean

Calories	80
Calories from Fat	20
Total Fat	2.0 g
Saturated Fat	1.2 g
Trans Fat	0.0 g
Cholesterol	25 mg
Sodium	360 mg
Potassium	310 mg
Total Carbohydrate	3 g
Dietary Fiber	2 g
Sugars	1 g
Protein	15 g
Phosphorus	150 mg

COOK'S TIP

Don't underestimate the importance of tossing the lettuce and dressing together first—it balances the recipe's flavors. The tuna packet works better in this recipe than canned tuna would—the packet tuna flakes perfectly over the well-dressed salad.

Seaside Shrimp Salad

SERVES 4 ■ **SERVING SIZE** rounded 1/2 cup ■ **PREP TIME** 6 minutes ■ **COOK TIME** 5 minutes
STAND TIME 10 minutes ■ **CHILL TIME** 2 hours

1 1/2 pounds peeled raw fresh or frozen and thawed shrimp

2 tablespoons reduced-fat mayonnaise

1 1/2 teaspoons seafood seasoning

6 tablespoons lemon juice

1. Bring water to boil in a large saucepan over high heat. Add the shrimp and return to a boil. Reduce the heat and simmer, uncovered, 2–3 minutes or until the shrimp is opaque in the center.

2. Drain the shrimp in a colander, rinse with cold water for 30 seconds, and pat dry with paper towels. Let stand 10 minutes to cool completely.

3. Place shrimp in a medium bowl with the mayonnaise, seafood seasoning, and lemon juice. Stir gently to coat. Cover with plastic wrap and refrigerate 2 hours. Serve as is or over tomato slices or lettuce leaves.

EXCHANGES / CHOICES

3 Protein, lean

Calories	130
Calories from Fat	20
Total Fat	2.0 g
Saturated Fat	0.3 g
Trans Fat	0.0 g
Cholesterol	205 mg
Sodium	430 mg
Potassium	310 mg
Total Carbohydrate	3 g
Dietary Fiber	0 g
Sugars	1 g
Protein	26 g
Phosphorus	260 mg

COOK'S TIP

For added lemon flavor, add 1/2 teaspoon lemon zest along with the lemon juice.

Ginger'd Ambrosia

SERVES 4 ■ **SERVING SIZE** 1/4 recipe ■ **PREP TIME** 12 minutes ■ **STAND TIME** 5–10 minutes

3 medium navel oranges, peeled and cut into bite-sized sections (about 1 1/2 cups total)

3 tablespoons flaked, sweetened, shredded coconut

2–3 teaspoons grated gingerroot

4 fresh or canned pineapple slices, packed in juice, drained

1 Place all ingredients except the pineapple in a medium bowl and toss gently. If desired, add 1 teaspoon pourable sugar substitute. Let stand 5–10 minutes to develop flavors.

2 Arrange each pineapple slice on a salad plate and spoon a rounded 1/3 cup of the orange mixture on each slice.

EXCHANGES / CHOICES

1 Fruit
1/2 Fat

Calories	80
Calories from Fat	15
Total Fat	1.5 g
Saturated Fat	1.4 g
Trans Fat	0.0 g
Cholesterol	0 mg
Sodium	10 mg
Potassium	200 mg
Total Carbohydrate	18 g
Dietary Fiber	3 g
Sugars	14 g
Protein	1 g
Phosphorus	20 mg

COOK'S TIP
You can find orange sections in the refrigerated produce section of your supermarket, but the degree of sweetness may vary slightly.

Zesty Citrus Melon

SERVES 4 ■ SERVING SIZE 3/4 cup ■ PREP TIME 5 minutes

1/4 cup orange juice

2–3 tablespoons lemon juice

1 teaspoon honey

3 cups diced honeydew or cantaloupe melon

1 Stir the orange juice, lemon zest (if using), lemon juice, and honey together in a small bowl.

2 Place the melon on a serving plate and pour the juice mixture evenly over all. For peak flavor, serve within 1 hour.

EXCHANGES / CHOICES
1 Fruit

Calories	60
Calories from Fat	0
Total Fat	0.0 g
Saturated Fat	0.1 g
Trans Fat	0.0 g
Cholesterol	0 mg
Sodium	25 mg
Potassium	330 mg
Total Carbohydrate	15 g
Dietary Fiber	1 g
Sugars	13 g
Protein	1 g
Phosphorus	15 mg

COOK'S TIP
Try using half cantaloupe and half honeydew in this recipe.

Toasted Pecan and Apple Salad

SERVES 4 ■ **SERVING SIZE** 1/2 cup ■ **PREP TIME** 8 minutes

2 tablespoons pecan chips

2 cups chopped unpeeled red apples

1/4 cup dried raisin-cherry blend (or 1/4 cup dried cherries or golden raisins alone)

1 teaspoon honey (or 1 teaspoon packed dark brown sugar and 1 teaspoon water)

1 Place a small skillet over medium-high heat until hot. Add the pecans and cook 1–2 minutes or until beginning to lightly brown, stirring constantly. Remove from the heat and set aside on paper towels to stop the cooking process and cool quickly.

2 Combine the apples and dried fruit in a medium bowl, drizzle honey over all, and toss gently.

3 Serve on a lettuce leaf (if desired) or a pretty salad plate. Sprinkle each serving evenly with the pecans.

EXCHANGES / CHOICES

1 Fruit
1/2 Fat

Calories	90
Calories from Fat	20
Total Fat	2.5 g
Saturated Fat	0.2 g
Trans Fat	0.0 g
Cholesterol	0 mg
Sodium	0 mg
Potassium	130 mg
Total Carbohydrate	18 g
Dietary Fiber	2 g
Sugars	14 g
Protein	1 g
Phosphorus	50 mg

COOK'S TIP

Using pecan chips rather than pieces makes the nutty flavors "stretch" further in the salad. If chips are unavailable, place pecan pieces in a small zippered plastic bag and crush slightly by tapping the pieces with the back of a heavy spoon. This releases the nutty flavor.

SOUPS

Chinese Starter Soup

SERVES 4 ■ **SERVING SIZE** 1 cup ■ **PREP TIME** 4 minutes
COOK TIME 10 minutes ■ **STAND TIME** 3 minutes

3 cups low-fat, low-sodium
  chicken broth

8 ounces frozen stir-fry vegetables,
  such as a mix of broccoli, carrots,
  water chestnuts, and onion

2 teaspoons grated gingerroot

2 teaspoons lite soy sauce

1 In a medium saucepan, bring the broth to boil over high heat. Add the vegetables and return to a boil.

2 Reduce the heat, cover tightly, and simmer 3–4 minutes or until vegetables are tender-crisp.

3 Remove from the heat and add the remaining ingredients. Top with red pepper flakes, if desired. Cover and let stand 3 minutes to develop flavors, then serve.

EXCHANGES / CHOICES
1 Nonstarchy Vegetable

Calories	50
Calories from Fat	0
Total Fat	0.0 g
Saturated Fat	0.0 g
Trans Fat	0.0 g
Cholesterol	0 mg
Sodium	210 mg
Potassium	280 mg
Total Carbohydrate	7 g
Dietary Fiber	1 g
Sugars	3 g
Protein	4 g
Phosphorus	90 mg

COOK'S TIP
This soup is best served immediately, when flavors and texture are at their peak.

Smoky Tomato Pepper Soup

SERVES 4 ■ **SERVING SIZE** 1 cup ■ **PREP TIME** 5 minutes ■ **COOK TIME** 32 minutes

1 (14.5-ounce) can no-salt-added stewed tomatoes

8 ounces frozen pepper and onion stir-fry

1/2–1 medium chipotle chili pepper in adobo sauce, mashed with a fork and then finely chopped (1 1/2 teaspoons to 1 tablespoon total)

1 cup water

1 (15.5-ounce) can navy beans, rinsed and drained

1. In a large saucepan, combine the tomatoes, peppers, chipotle pepper, and water. Bring to a boil over high heat.

2. Reduce the heat, cover tightly, and simmer 25 minutes or until onions are tender, stirring occasionally.

3. Mash the larger pieces of tomato with a fork, then add the beans and 1/4 teaspoon salt, if desired and cook 5 minutes longer.

EXCHANGES / CHOICES

1 Starch
2 Nonstarchy Vegetable

Calories	130
Calories from Fat	10
Total Fat	1.0 g
Saturated Fat	0.1 g
Trans Fat	0.0 g
Cholesterol	0 mg
Sodium	190 mg
Potassium	530 mg
Total Carbohydrate	26 g
Dietary Fiber	9 g
Sugars	7 g
Protein	6 g
Phosphorus	120 mg

COOK'S TIP

This is a very spicy dish made with half a chipotle pepper— for a milder flavor, use less.

Very Veggie Soup

SERVES 4 ■ **SERVING SIZE** 1 cup ■ **PREP TIME** 2 minutes
COOK TIME 15 minutes ■ **STAND TIME** 5 minutes

4 ounces reduced-fat pork breakfast sausage

2 cups coarsely chopped green cabbage (about 3/4-inch pieces)

1 (10-ounce) package frozen mixed vegetables

1 (14.5-ounce) can stewed tomatoes with liquid

1 1/2 cups water

1 Place a large saucepan over medium-high heat until hot. Coat pan with nonstick cooking spray and add the sausage. Cook the sausage until no longer pink, stirring constantly, breaking up large pieces while cooking. Set aside on separate plate.

2 Recoat the pan with nonstick cooking spray, add the cabbage, and cook 3 minutes, stirring frequently. Add the remaining ingredients and bring to a boil. Reduce the heat, cover tightly, and simmer 10 minutes or until vegetables are tender.

3 Remove from the heat, stir in the sausage, cover, and let stand 5 minutes to develop flavors.

EXCHANGES / CHOICES

4 Nonstarchy Vegetable
1 Fat

Calories	150
Calories from Fat	40
Total Fat	4.5 g
Saturated Fat	1.5 g
Trans Fat	0.1 g
Cholesterol	15 mg
Sodium	330 mg
Potassium	470 mg
Total Carbohydrate	19 g
Dietary Fiber	5 g
Sugars	8 g
Protein	8 g
Phosphorus	105 mg

COOK'S TIP

This is a great recipe to double and freeze in 1-cup quantities for a quick meal. Reheat in the microwave on HIGH for 3 minutes, stir, and cook 1 minute longer or until thoroughly heated.

Green Pepper Skillet Chili

SERVES 4 ■ **SERVING SIZE** 3/4 cup ■ **PREP TIME** 5 minutes
COOK TIME 25 minutes ■ **STAND TIME** 10 minutes

1 pound 93% lean ground beef

1 large green bell pepper, chopped (about 1 1/2 cups total)

1 (14.5-ounce) can stewed no-added-salt tomatoes with liquid

1 (1.25-ounce) packet chili seasoning mix

3/4 cup water

1. Place a large nonstick skillet over medium-high heat until hot. Coat the skillet with nonstick cooking spray, add the beef, and cook until no longer pink, stirring frequently. Set aside on a separate plate.

2. Recoat the skillet with nonstick cooking spray, add the peppers, and cook 5 minutes or until the edges begin to brown, stirring frequently.

3. Add the remaining ingredients to the skillet and bring to a boil. Reduce the heat, cover tightly, and simmer 15 minutes or until peppers are very tender, stirring occasionally, using the back of a spoon to crush the tomatoes while cooking.

4. Remove from the heat and let stand 10 minutes to develop flavors.

EXCHANGES / CHOICES

1/2 Carbohydrate
2 Nonstarchy Vegetable
1 Protein, lean
1/2 Fat

Calories	150
Calories from Fat	45
Total Fat	5.0 g
Saturated Fat	1.6 g
Trans Fat	0.2 g
Cholesterol	35 mg
Sodium	390 mg
Potassium	620 mg
Total Carbohydrate	16 g
Dietary Fiber	3 g
Sugars	7 g
Protein	13 g
Phosphorus	135 mg

COOK'S TIP

Be sure to use the stewed variety of tomatoes in this recipe—their sweetness cuts the acidity of the tomatoes and provides additional flavor.

Sweet Corn and Peppers Soup

SERVES 5 ■ **SERVING SIZE** 1 cup ■ **PREP TIME** 5 minutes
COOK TIME 20 minutes ■ **STAND TIME** 5 minutes

1 cup water

1 pound frozen pepper and onion stir-fry

10 ounces frozen corn kernels, thawed

1 1/4 cups fat-free milk

2 ounces reduced-fat processed cheese
(such as Velveeta), cut in small cubes

1/8 teaspoon black pepper

1. In a large saucepan, bring the water to boil over high heat. Add the peppers and return to a boil. Reduce the heat, cover tightly, and simmer 15 minutes or until onions are tender.

2. Add the corn and milk. Increase the heat to high, bring just to a boil, and remove from the heat.

3. Add the remaining ingredients and 1/2 teaspoon salt, if desired, cover, and let stand 5 minutes to melt the cheese and develop flavors.

EXCHANGES / CHOICES

1 Starch
1 Nonstarchy Vegetable
1/2 Fat

Calories	120
Calories from Fat	20
Total Fat	2.0 g
Saturated Fat	0.9 g
Trans Fat	0.0 g
Cholesterol	5 mg
Sodium	220 mg
Potassium	360 mg
Total Carbohydrate	21 g
Dietary Fiber	3 g
Sugars	10 g
Protein	6 g
Phosphorus	240 mg

COOK'S TIP

Be sure to add the cheese after you've removed the saucepan from the heat; otherwise, the cheese will curdle.

Creamy Potato Soup with Green Onions

SERVES 3 ■ **SERVING SIZE** 1 cup ■ **PREP TIME** 10 minutes ■ **COOK TIME** 15 minutes

2 cups fat-free milk

1 pound baking potatoes, peeled and diced

3 tablespoons no-trans-fat margarine (35% vegetable oil)

1/4 teaspoon salt

1/4 teaspoon black pepper

3 tablespoons finely chopped green onions, green and white parts

1 Bring the milk just to a boil in a large saucepan over high heat (catch it before it comes to a full boil).

2 Add the potatoes and return just to a boil. Reduce the heat, cover tightly, and simmer 12 minutes or until the potatoes are tender.

3 Remove from the heat and add the margarine, salt, and pepper. Using a whisk or potato masher or handheld electric mixer, mash the mixture until thickened, but still lumpy.

4 Spoon into individual bowls and sprinkle each serving with 1 tablespoon onions.

EXCHANGES / CHOICES

1 1/2 Starch
1/2 Milk, fat-free
1 Fat

Calories	200
Calories from Fat	45
Total Fat	5.0 g
Saturated Fat	1.2 g
Trans Fat	0.0 g
Cholesterol	5 mg
Sodium	360 mg
Potassium	660 mg
Total Carbohydrate	32 g
Dietary Fiber	2 g
Sugars	9 g
Protein	8 g
Phosphorus	215 mg

COOK'S TIP

For a more colorful soup, use Yukon Gold potatoes.

Tilapia Stew with Green Peppers

SERVES 4 ■ **SERVING SIZE** 1 cup ■ **PREP TIME** 10 minutes
COOK TIME 40 minutes ■ **STAND TIME** 10 minutes

1 medium green bell pepper, chopped

1 (14.5-ounce) can stewed tomatoes
with Italian seasonings

1 cup water

1 pound tilapia filets, rinsed and cut into
1-inch pieces

1/2 teaspoon seafood seasoning

1. Place a large saucepan over medium heat until hot.
Coat the pan with nonstick cooking spray, add the
bell pepper, and cook 5 minutes or until beginning to
lightly brown, stirring frequently.

2. Add the tomatoes and water, increase to high heat,
and bring to a boil. Reduce the heat, cover tightly, and
simmer until the tomatoes are tender. Using the back
of a spoon, break up the larger pieces of tomato.

3. Add the fish and seasonings and stir very gently.
Increase the heat to high and bring just to a boil.
Reduce the heat, cover tightly, and simmer 3 minutes
or until the fish is opaque in the center. Remove from
the heat and let stand, covered, 10 minutes to develop
flavors.

EXCHANGES / CHOICES

2 Nonstarchy Vegetable
3 Protein, lean

Calories	150
Calories from Fat	20
Total Fat	2.0 g
Saturated Fat	0.7 g
Trans Fat	0.0 g
Cholesterol	55 mg
Sodium	350 mg
Potassium	620 mg
Total Carbohydrate	10 g
Dietary Fiber	2 g
Sugars	6 g
Protein	24 g
Phosphorus	220 mg

COOK'S TIP

Be careful not to over stir the stew after adding the fish, or it
will flake too much and change the texture and appearance
of the stew.

POULTRY

Chicken Apple Sausage and Onion Smothered Grits

SERVES 4 ■ **SERVING SIZE** 3/4 cup sausage mixture and about 1/2 cup cooked grits
PREP TIME 5 minutes ■ **COOK TIME** 10 minutes

2/3 cup dry quick cooking grits

8 ounces sliced fresh mushrooms

3 (4 ounces each) links fully cooked chicken apple sausage, thinly sliced, such as Al Fresco

1 1/2 cups chopped onion

1. Bring 2 2/3 cups water to a boil in a medium saucepan. Slowly stir in the grits, reduce heat to medium-low, cover, and cook 5–7 minutes or until thickened.

2. Meanwhile, heat a large skillet coated with cooking spray over medium-high heat. Add the mushrooms and cook 4 minutes or until beginning to lightly brown. Set aside on separate plate.

3. Coat skillet with cooking spray and cook sausage 3 minutes or until browned on edges, stirring occasionally. Set aside with mushrooms. To pan residue, add onions, coat with cooking spray, and cook 4 minutes or until richly browned. Add the sausage and mushrooms back to the skillet with any accumulated juices and 1/4 cup water. Cook 1 minute to heat through.

4. Sprinkle with 1/8 teaspoon salt and 1/8 teaspoon pepper. Spoon equal amounts of the grits in each of 4 shallow soup bowls, top with the sausage mixture.

EXCHANGES / CHOICES

1 Vegetable
1 1/2 Starch
3 Protein, lean

Calories	270
Calories from Fat	60
Total Fat	7 g
Saturated Fat	1.6 g
Trans Fat	0.0 g
Cholesterol	60 mg
Sodium	430 mg
Potassium	565 mg
Total Carbohydrate	31 g
Dietary Fiber	3 g
Sugars	4 g
Protein	19 g
Phosphorus	235 mg

COOK'S TIP
May replace grits with quinoa, if desired.

Avocado and Green Chili Chicken

SERVES 4 ■ **SERVING SIZE** 3 ounces cooked chicken and 1/4 cup avocado
PREP TIME 5 minutes ■ **COOK TIME** 22 minutes

4 (4 ounces each) boneless, skinless chicken breast, flattened to 1/2-inch thickness

1 (4-ounce) can chopped mild green chilies

1 ripe medium avocado, chopped

1 lime, halved

1 Preheat oven to 400°F.

2 Place chicken in an 11 × 7-inch baking pan, squeeze half of the lime over all. Spoon green chilies on top of each breast and spread over all. Bake, uncovered, 22–25 minutes or until chicken is no longer pink in center.

3 Top with avocado, squeeze remaining lime half over all, and sprinkle evenly with 1/4 teaspoon salt and 1/4 teaspoon pepper.

EXCHANGES / CHOICES

1 Nonstarchy Vegetable
3 Protein, lean
1 Fat

Calories	200
Calories from Fat	70
Total Fat	8 g
Saturated Fat	1.4 g
Trans Fat	0.0 g
Cholesterol	85 mg
Sodium	310 mg
Potassium	720 mg
Total Carbohydrate	6 g
Dietary Fiber	3 g
Sugars	1 g
Protein	27 g
Phosphorus	265 mg

COOK'S TIP

For added color, add 1/2 cup quartered grape tomatoes with the avocado.

Panko Ranch Chicken Strips with Dipping Sauce

SERVES 4 ■ **SERVING SIZE** 2 chicken tenderloins and 2 tablespoons sauce
PREP TIME 10 minutes ■ **COOK TIME** 12 minutes

8 chicken tenderloins, about 1 pound total

3/4 cup yogurt ranch dressing, divided use

3/4 cup panko breadcrumbs

3 tablespoons canola oil

1. Place chicken in a medium bowl with 1/4 cup of the ranch dressing; toss until well coated. Place the breadcrumbs in a shallow pan, such as a pie pan. Coat chicken pieces, one at a time with the breadcrumbs and set aside.

2. Heat oil in a large skillet over medium-high heat. Add the chicken and immediately reduce to medium-low heat, cook 12 minutes or until golden and no longer pink in center, gently turning occasionally.

3. Remove from skillet, sprinkle with 1/8 teaspoon salt. Serve with remaining 1/2 cup ranch for dipping.

EXCHANGES / CHOICES

1 Starch
3 1/2 Protein, lean
2 Fat

Calories	340
Calories from Fat	140
Total Fat	16.0 g
Saturated Fat	2.5 g
Trans Fat	0.0 g
Cholesterol	85 mg
Sodium	390 mg
Potassium	485 mg
Total Carbohydrate	17 g
Dietary Fiber	1 g
Sugars	4 g
Protein	30 g
Phosphorus	310 mg

Sausage and Farro Mushrooms

SERVES 4 ■ **SERVING SIZE** 2 mushroom caps and 1/2 cup sausage mixture
PREP TIME 5 minutes ■ **COOK TIME** 20 minutes

1/2 cup dry pearled farro

2 (3.9 ounces each) Italian turkey sausage links, removed from casing, such as Jennie-o

8 portabella mushroom caps, stems removed, caps wiped with damp cloth

2 tablespoons crumbled reduced-fat blue cheese

1 Preheat broiler. Coat both sides of the mushrooms with cooking spray, place on a foil-lined baking sheet, and broil 5 minutes on each side or until tender.

2 Meanwhile, heat a large nonstick skillet over medium-high heat, add sausage, and cook 3 minutes or until browned, breaking up larger pieces while cooking. Set aside on separate plate.

3 Add 2 cups water and the farro to any pan residue in skillet, bring to a boil, reduce heat to medium-low, cover, and simmer 15 minutes or until slightly "chewy." Stir in the sausage and cheese; cook, uncovered, for 2 minutes to thicken slightly. Spoon equal amounts into each mushroom cap and sprinkle with black pepper.

EXCHANGES / CHOICES

1 Starch
1 Nonstarchy Vegetable
2 Protein, lean
1/2 Fat

Calories	200
Calories from Fat	50
Total Fat	6.0 g
Saturated Fat	1.8 g
Trans Fat	0.2 g
Cholesterol	30 mg
Sodium	390 mg
Potassium	710 mg
Total Carbohydrate	23 g
Dietary Fiber	3 g
Sugars	2 g
Protein	16 g
Phosphorus	310 mg

COOK'S TIP

Be sure to add the black pepper to tie all the flavors together!

COOK'S TIP

Farro is one of the oldest grains and is grown in Italy. It is a great source of fiber and protein.

Turkey Patties with Dark Onion Gravy

SERVES 4 ■ **SERVING SIZE** 3 ounces cooked turkey and 1/4 cup onion gravy
PREP TIME 10 minutes ■ **COOK TIME** 20 minutes

1 pound 93% lean ground turkey

1 tablespoon flour

1 1/3 cups chopped yellow onion

1 tablespoon sodium-free chicken bouillon granules

1. Shape the turkey into 4 patties, about 1/2 inch thick; sprinkle with 1/8 teaspoon salt and 1/8 teaspoon pepper, if desired.

2. Heat a large skillet over medium-high heat. Add flour and cook 3 minutes or until beginning to lightly brown, stirring constantly. Set aside on separate plate.

3. Coat skillet with cooking spray, add onions, and cook 3 minutes or until beginning to brown on edges. Push to one side of the skillet, add the turkey patties, reduce to medium heat, and cook 6 minutes on each side or until no longer pink in center.

4. Remove the turkey patties from the onion mixture and set aside on serving platter. Add 1 cup water and bouillon granules to the onions, sprinkle with the flour and 1/8 teaspoon salt and 1/8 teaspoon pepper. Stir and cook until thickened, about 1 1/2 to 2 minutes. Spoon over patties.

EXCHANGES / CHOICES

2 Nonstarchy Vegetables
3 1/2 Protein, lean

Calories	210
Calories from Fat	90
Total Fat	10.0 g
Saturated Fat	2.5 g
Trans Fat	0.0 g
Cholesterol	84 mg
Sodium	230 mg
Potassium	330 mg
Total Carbohydrate	8 g
Dietary Fiber	1 g
Sugars	2 g
Protein	22 g
Phosphorus	240 mg

Rustic Mexican Chicken and Rice

SERVES 4 ■ **SERVING SIZE** 1 1/4 cups ■ **PREP TIME** 5 minutes ■ **COOK TIME** 8 hours

1 pound boneless, skinless chicken thighs, trimmed of fat

1 (10-ounce) can diced tomatoes with green chilies

3/4 cup instant brown rice

2 tablespoons extra-virgin olive oil

1 Combine chicken and tomatoes in a 3 1/2 to 4-quart slow cooker, cover, and cook on low setting for 7–8 hours or on high setting for 3 1/2–4 hours.

2 Gently stir in rice and 3/4 cup hot water, cover, and cook on high for 20 minutes.

3 Drizzle oil evenly over all and sprinkle with 1/8 teaspoon salt.

EXCHANGES / CHOICES

1 Nonstarchy Vegetable
1/2 Starch
3 1/2 Protein, lean
1/2 Fat

Calories	250
Calories from Fat	110
Total Fat	12.0 g
Saturated Fat	2.3 g
Trans Fat	0.0 g
Cholesterol	110 mg
Sodium	510 mg
Potassium	365 mg
Total Carbohydrate	12 g
Dietary Fiber	1 g
Sugars	0 g
Protein	24 g
Phosphorus	250 mg

Panko Ranch Chicken Strips
with Dipping Sauce
page 87

Peach Barbecued Chicken

SERVES 4 ■ **SERVING SIZE** 2 drumsticks ■ **PREP TIME** 15 minutes ■ **COOK TIME** 18 minutes

8 chicken drumsticks, skin removed, rinsed and patted dry (about 2 pounds total)

2 tablespoons peach all-fruit spread

1/4 cup barbeque sauce, preferably hickory- or mesquite-flavored

2 teaspoons grated gingerroot

1 Preheat the broiler.

2 Coat a broiler rack and pan with nonstick cooking spray. Arrange the drumsticks on the rack and broil about 4 inches away from heat source for 8 minutes. Turn and broil 6 minutes or until the juices run clear.

3 Meanwhile, place the fruit spread in a small glass bowl and microwave on HIGH 20 seconds or until the fruit spread has melted slightly. Add the barbeque sauce and ginger and stir to blend. Place 1 tablespoon of the mixture in a separate small bowl and set aside.

4 When the chicken is cooked, brush with half of the sauce and broil 2 minutes. Turn the drumsticks, brush with the remaining half of the sauce, and broil 2 more minutes.

5 Remove the drumsticks from the broiler, turn them over, and brush with the reserved 1 tablespoon sauce to serve.

EXCHANGES / CHOICES

1 Carbohydrate
4 Protein, lean

Calories	230
Calories from Fat	50
Total Fat	6.0 g
Saturated Fat	1.5 g
Trans Fat	0.0 g
Cholesterol	95 mg
Sodium	220 mg
Potassium	300 mg
Total Carbohydrate	13 g
Dietary Fiber	0 g
Sugars	10 g
Protein	29 g
Phosphorus	195 mg

COOK'S TIP

For easy cleanup, line the broiler rack and pan with foil and cut slits in the foil to allow the grease to drip down onto the broiler pan.

Greek Chicken with Lemon

SERVES 4 ■ **SERVING SIZE** 2 drumsticks ■ **PREP TIME** 15 minutes
MARINATE TIME 8 hours ■ **COOK TIME** 50 minutes

8 chicken drumsticks, skin removed, rinsed and patted dry

2 tablespoons dried salt-free Greek seasoning (sold in jars in the spice aisle)

2 teaspoons extra virgin olive oil

1 teaspoon lemon zest

4 tablespoons lemon juice (divided use)

1. Place the drumsticks, Greek seasoning, olive oil, lemon zest, and 2 tablespoons lemon juice in a gallon-sized zippered plastic bag. Seal the bag and toss back and forth to coat the chicken evenly. Refrigerate for 8 hours or up to 48 hours, turning occasionally.

2. Preheat the oven to 350°F.

3. Coat a 12 × 8-inch baking dish with nonstick cooking spray, arrange the drumsticks in a single layer, and pour the marinade evenly over all. Bake uncovered for 50–55 minutes or until the drumsticks are no longer pink in the center, turning occasionally.

4. Place the drumsticks on a serving platter. Add salt to taste, if desired, and 2 tablespoons lemon juice to a small bowl, stir to blend well, and pour evenly over the chicken pieces. Season with 1/8 teaspoon salt, if desired.

EXCHANGES / CHOICES

4 Protein, lean
1/2 Fat

Calories	210
Calories from Fat	70
Total Fat	8.0 g
Saturated Fat	1.9 g
Trans Fat	0.0 g
Cholesterol	95 mg
Sodium	100 mg
Potassium	300 mg
Total Carbohydrate	2 g
Dietary Fiber	1 g
Sugars	0 g
Protein	30 g
Phosphorus	195 mg

COOK'S TIP

To skin the drumsticks easily and quickly, use one paper towel per drumstick. Grab the skin with the paper towel and pull. You'll get great traction and the chicken skin won't slip between your fingers!

Taco Chicken Tenders

SERVES 4 ■ **SERVING SIZE** 3 ounces ■ **PREP TIME** 5 minutes
COOK TIME 7 minutes ■ **STAND TIME** 1 minute

4 teaspoons taco seasoning mix
(available in packets)

1 pound chicken tenderloins, rinsed and
patted dry

1/2 medium lime

2 tablespoons fat-free sour cream

1   Sprinkle the taco seasoning evenly over both sides of the chicken pieces, pressing down gently so the spices adhere.

2   Place a large nonstick skillet over medium-high heat until hot. Coat the skillet with nonstick cooking spray, add the chicken, and cook 2 minutes.

3   Turn gently to keep the seasonings on the chicken as much as possible, reduce the heat to medium, and cook 2 minutes. Turn gently and cook 2 more minutes or until the chicken is no longer pink in the center.

4   Remove from the heat, squeeze lime juice evenly over all, and serve with 1/2 tablespoon sour cream per serving.

EXCHANGES / CHOICES
3 Protein, lean

Calories	140
Calories from Fat	25
Total Fat	3.0 g
Saturated Fat	0.8 g
Trans Fat	0.0 g
Cholesterol	65 mg
Sodium	290 mg
Potassium	220 mg
Total Carbohydrate	3 g
Dietary Fiber	1 g
Sugars	1 g
Protein	24 g
Phosphorus	195 mg

COOK'S TIP
Store the remaining taco seasoning mix in a small zippered plastic bag in the pantry for later use.

Dijon'd Chicken with Rosemary

SERVES 4 ■ **SERVING SIZE** 3 ounces ■ **PREP TIME** 5 minutes ■ **COOK TIME** 13 minutes

1 tablespoon Dijon mustard

1 tablespoon extra virgin olive oil

1/4 teaspoon dried rosemary

4 (4-ounce) boneless, skinless chicken
   breasts, rinsed and patted dry

1   Using a fork, stir the mustard, olive oil, and rosemary together in a small bowl until well blended and set aside.

2   Place a medium nonstick skillet over medium heat until hot. Coat the skillet with nonstick cooking spray, add the chicken, and cook 5 minutes.

3   Turn the chicken, then spoon equal amounts of the mustard mixture over each piece. Reduce the heat to medium low, cover tightly, and cook 7 minutes or until the chicken is no longer pink in the center.

4   Turn the chicken several times to blend the mustard mixture with the pan drippings, place the chicken on a serving platter, and spoon the mustard mixture over all.

EXCHANGES / CHOICES

3 Protein, lean
1/2 Fat

Calories	160
Calories from Fat	50
Total Fat	6.0 g
Saturated Fat	1.2 g
Trans Fat	0.0 g
Cholesterol	65 mg
Sodium	150 mg
Potassium	200 mg
Total Carbohydrate	1 g
Dietary Fiber	0 g
Sugars	0 g
Protein	24 g
Phosphorus	175 mg

COOK'S TIP

For a more flavorful dish, crush the rosemary leaves before adding them to the mustard and oil.

Cheesy Chicken and Rice

SERVES 4 ■ **SERVING SIZE** 1 1/2 cups ■ **PREP TIME** 10 minutes ■ **COOK TIME** 12 minutes

1 1/2 cups water

1 cup instant brown rice

12 ounces frozen broccoli and cauliflower florets

12 ounces boneless, skinless chicken breast, rinsed and patted dry, cut into bite-sized pieces

3 ounces reduced-fat processed cheese (such as Velveeta), cut in 1/2-inch cubes

1 Bring the water to boil in a large saucepan, then add the rice and vegetables. Return to a boil, reduce the heat, cover tightly, and simmer 10 minutes or until the liquid is absorbed.

2 Meanwhile, place a large nonstick skillet over medium heat until hot. Coat the skillet with nonstick cooking spray and add the chicken. Cook 10 minutes or until the chicken is no longer pink in the center and is just beginning to lightly brown on the edges, stirring frequently.

3 Add the chicken, cheese, 1/8 teaspoon salt, if desired, and pepper to the rice mixture and stir until the cheese has melted. Add pepper to taste, if desired.

EXCHANGES / CHOICES
2 1/2 Starch
1 Nonstarchy Vegetable
3 Protein, lean

Calories	340
Calories from Fat	50
Total Fat	6.0 g
Saturated Fat	1.9 g
Trans Fat	0.0 g
Cholesterol	55 mg
Sodium	380 mg
Potassium	440 mg
Total Carbohydrate	43 g
Dietary Fiber	4 g
Sugars	4 g
Protein	28 g
Phosphorus	525 mg

Molasses Drumsticks
with Soy Sauce

SERVES 4 ■ **SERVING SIZE** 2 drumsticks ■ **PREP TIME** 10 minutes
MARINATE TIME 2 hours ■ **COOK TIME** 25 minutes ■ **STAND TIME** 3 minutes

2 1/2 tablespoons lite soy sauce

1 1/4 tablespoons lime juice

8 chicken drumsticks, skin removed, rinsed, and patted dry

2 tablespoons dark molasses

1 Stir the soy sauce and lime juice together in a small bowl until well blended.

2 Place the drumsticks in a large zippered plastic bag. Add 2 tablespoons of the soy sauce mixture to the bag. Seal tightly and shake back and forth to coat chicken evenly. Refrigerate overnight or at least 2 hours, turning occasionally.

3 Add the molasses to the remaining soy sauce mixture, cover with plastic wrap, and refrigerate until needed.

4 Preheat the broiler. Lightly coat the broiler rack and pan with nonstick cooking spray, place the drumsticks on the rack, and discard any marinade in the bag. Broil 6 inches away from the heat source for 25 minutes, turning every 5 minutes or until the drumsticks are no longer pink in the center.

5 Place the drumsticks in a large bowl. Stir the reserved soy sauce mixture and pour it over the drumsticks. Toss the drumsticks gently to coat evenly and let them stand 3 minutes to develop flavors.

EXCHANGES / CHOICES

1/2 Carbohydrate
4 Protein, lean

Calories	210
Calories from Fat	50
Total Fat	6.0 g
Saturated Fat	1.5 g
Trans Fat	0.0 g
Cholesterol	95 mg
Sodium	450 mg
Potassium	370 mg
Total Carbohydrate	6 g
Dietary Fiber	0 g
Sugars	4 g
Protein	30 g
Phosphorus	205 mg

COOK'S TIP
These drumsticks are best served immediately.

Country Roast Chicken with Lemony Au Jus

SERVES 6 ■ SERVING SIZE 3 ounces ■ PREP TIME 20 minutes
COOK TIME 1 hour and 20 minutes ■ STAND TIME 15–20 minutes

3 1/2-pound roasting chicken, rinsed and patted dry, including the cavity

2 medium lemons, quartered

3/4 teaspoon poultry seasoning

3/4 teaspoon garlic powder

3/4 teaspoon salt

1/4 teaspoon black pepper

2 cups water

1. Preheat the oven to 425°F.

2. Coat a broiler rack and pan with nonstick cooking spray. Place the chicken on the rack. Squeeze the lemons evenly over the chicken and place the lemon rinds in the cavity of the chicken.

3. Combine the poultry seasoning, garlic powder, salt, and pepper in a small bowl. Blend well and sprinkle evenly over the chicken. Place the chicken in the oven, pour the water through the slits of the broiler pan, and cook 30 minutes.

4. Reduce the heat to 375°F and cook 50–55 minutes or until a meat thermometer reaches 180°F. Remove the chicken from the oven and let it stand on the broiler rack for 10 minutes.

5. Place the chicken on a cutting board. Carefully pour the pan drippings into a grease separator or a plastic zippered bag. Freeze the drippings for 10 minutes to separate the grease.

6. Remove the grease from the separator or bag, pour drippings into a glass dish, and heat in the microwave on HIGH for 30 seconds. Slice the chicken, discarding the skin, and serve with the drippings.

EXCHANGES / CHOICES

3 Protein, lean
1/2 Fat

Calories	160
Calories from Fat	50
Total Fat	6.0 g
Saturated Fat	1.7 g
Trans Fat	0.0 g
Cholesterol	75 mg
Sodium	220 mg
Potassium	220 mg
Total Carbohydrate	1 g
Dietary Fiber	0 g
Sugars	0 g
Protein	25 g
Phosphorus	170 mg

COOK'S TIP

To separate the grease: pour pan drippings into a measuring cup, then into the bag. Hold the bag over a small bowl or saucepan, snip off a bottom corner of the bag, and allow the juice to run out.

Seared Chicken with Spicy Chipotle Cream Sauce

SERVES 4 ■ **SERVING SIZE** 3 ounces ■ **PREP TIME** 8 minutes ■ **COOK TIME** 14 minutes

4 (4-ounce) boneless, skinless chicken breasts, rinsed and patted dry

1/2 teaspoon salt (divided use)

1/3 cup water

6 tablespoons fat-free sour cream

2 tablespoons reduced-fat mayonnaise

1/4–1/2 medium chipotle chili pepper in adobo sauce, mashed with a fork and then finely chopped (3/4 teaspoon to 1 1/2 teaspoons total)

1. Season the chicken with 1/4 teaspoon salt. Place a large nonstick skillet over medium-high heat until hot. Coat the skillet with nonstick cooking spray, add the chicken (smooth side down), and cook 3 minutes or until beginning to richly brown.

2. Turn the chicken and pour the water around the chicken pieces. Reduce the heat to medium, cover tightly, and cook 10 minutes or until the chicken is no longer pink in the center.

3. Meanwhile, stir the sour cream, mayonnaise, chipotle pepper, and 1/4 teaspoon salt together in a small bowl.

4. Remove the skillet from the heat and place the chicken on a serving platter. Cover the chicken with foil to keep warm.

5. Reduce the heat to medium low and return the skillet to the stove. Add the sour cream mixture and stir until well blended. Cook 1 minute or until thoroughly heated, stirring constantly. Be careful not to bring the sauce to a boil, or it will separate. Spoon about 2 tablespoons of sauce over each chicken breast to serve.

EXCHANGES / CHOICES

1/2 Carbohydrate
3 Protein, lean

Calories	170
Calories from Fat	40
Total Fat	4.5 g
Saturated Fat	1.1 g
Trans Fat	0.0 g
Cholesterol	70 mg
Sodium	440 mg
Potassium	230 mg
Total Carbohydrate	5 g
Dietary Fiber	0 g
Sugars	1 g
Protein	25 g
Phosphorus	200 mg

COOK'S TIP

This is a very spicy dish made with half a chipotle pepper—for a milder flavor, use less.

White Wine'd Chicken and Mushrooms

SERVES 4 ■ **SERVING SIZE** 3 ounces chicken plus 1/4 cup mushrooms
PREP TIME 5 minutes ■ **COOK TIME** 25 minutes

1 cup sliced mushrooms

1/4 teaspoon salt (divided use)

4 (4-ounce) boneless, skinless chicken breasts, rinsed and patted dry

1/8 teaspoon black pepper

1/2 cup dry white wine

2 tablespoons no-trans-fat margarine (35% vegetable oil)

1 Place a large nonstick skillet over medium-high heat until hot. Coat the skillet with nonstick cooking spray and add the mushrooms and 1/8 teaspoon salt. Cook for 5 minutes or until the mushrooms begin to richly brown on the edges, stirring frequently. Set the mushrooms aside on a separate plate.

2 Sprinkle the chicken with the remaining 1/8 teaspoon salt, pepper, and 1/8 teaspoon rosemary, if desired. Recoat the skillet with nonstick cooking spray and place the chicken in the skillet, smooth side down. Cook for 3 minutes, turn, and add the mushrooms and wine.

3 Bring the mixture to a boil, reduce the heat, cover tightly, and simmer 10 minutes or until the chicken is no longer pink in the center. Remove the chicken only, shaking off any mushrooms, and set it aside on a serving platter. Cover it with foil to keep warm.

4 Increase the heat to medium high, bring the mushroom mixture to a boil, and continue to boil 2–3 minutes or until most of the liquid has evaporated. Remove from the heat, stir in the margarine, and spoon over the chicken.

EXCHANGES / CHOICES
3 Protein, lean
1/2 Fat

Calories	160
Calories from Fat	45
Total Fat	5.0 g
Saturated Fat	1.3 g
Trans Fat	0.0 g
Cholesterol	65 mg
Sodium	250 mg
Potassium	260 mg
Total Carbohydrate	1 g
Dietary Fiber	0 g
Sugars	0 g
Protein	24 g
Phosphorus	190 mg

COOK'S TIP
Be sure to pat the chicken very dry with paper towels, or it won't brown properly.

Tangy Chicken and Peppers

SERVES 4 ■ **SERVING SIZE** 2 drumsticks plus 1/2 cup peppers ■ **PREP TIME** 15 minutes
COOK TIME 42 minutes ■ **STAND TIME** 5 minutes

8 chicken drumsticks, skin removed, rinsed and patted dry

1 large green bell pepper, thinly sliced

1 medium onion, thinly sliced

1 cup water

1/2 teaspoon salt (divided use)

1/8 teaspoon black pepper

1/4 cup no-salt-added ketchup

1 Place a large nonstick skillet over medium-high heat until hot. Coat the skillet with nonstick cooking spray, add the drumsticks, and cook 8 minutes or until the drumsticks begin to brown, turning occasionally. Set the drumsticks aside on a separate plate.

2 Recoat the skillet and pan residue with nonstick cooking spray and reduce the heat to medium. Add the peppers and onions and cook 3 minutes, or until they begin to lightly brown on the edges, stirring frequently.

3 Add the drumsticks and plate juices, water, 1/4 teaspoon salt, and pepper to the skillet. Increase the heat to high and bring to a boil. Reduce the heat, cover tightly, and simmer 30–35 minutes or until the drumsticks are no longer pink in the center, turning occasionally.

4 Place the drumsticks in a shallow pasta bowl or rimmed serving platter. Add the ketchup and 1/4 teaspoon salt to the pepper mixture in the skillet. Increase the heat to high, bring to a boil, and continue boiling 1 minute or until the mixture is reduced to 2 cups. Spoon the pepper mixture over the drumsticks, cover, and let stand 5 minutes to develop flavors.

EXCHANGES / CHOICES

2 Nonstarchy Vegetable
4 Protein, lean

Calories	220
Calories from Fat	50
Total Fat	6.0 g
Saturated Fat	1.6 g
Trans Fat	0.0 g
Cholesterol	95 mg
Sodium	400 mg
Potassium	460 mg
Total Carbohydrate	11 g
Dietary Fiber	2 g
Sugars	7 g
Protein	30 g
Phosphorus	215 mg

COOK'S TIP

To skin the drumsticks easily and quickly, use one paper towel per drumstick. Grab the skin with the paper towel and pull. You'll get great traction and the chicken skin won't slip between your fingers!

Chili'd Turkey Breast Au Jus

SERVES 12 ■ **SERVING SIZE** 4 ounces ■ **PREP TIME** 20 minutes
COOK TIME 1 hour and 45 minutes ■ **STAND TIME** 20 minutes

1 1/2 teaspoons chili powder

3/4 teaspoon dried sage

1/2 teaspoon dried rosemary

1/2 teaspoon black pepper

3/4 teaspoon salt (divided use)

6-pound frozen turkey breast with bone in, thawed, rinsed, and patted dry

2/3 cup cold water

1. Preheat the oven to 325°F.

2. Stir the chili powder, sage, rosemary, pepper, and 1/2 teaspoon salt together in a small bowl until well blended. Loosen the skin on the turkey breast by sliding your fingertips between the skin and the turkey meat (do not remove skin). Rub the chili mixture on the turkey meat under the skin.

3. Coat a 13 × 9-inch baking rack and pan with nonstick cooking spray, place the turkey on the baking rack, and bake 1 hour and 45 minutes or until a meat thermometer reaches 165°F. Place the turkey on a cutting board and let stand 20 minutes.

4. Meanwhile, add the water and remaining 1/4 teaspoon salt to the pan drippings and stir until well blended. Carefully pour the pan drippings into a grease separator or a plastic zippered bag. Freeze the drippings for 10 minutes to separate the grease.

5. Remove the grease from the separator or bag, pour drippings into a glass dish, and heat in the microwave on HIGH for 30 seconds. Slice the turkey, discard the skin, and serve with the drippings.

EXCHANGES / CHOICES

4 Protein, lean

Calories	180
Calories from Fat	10
Total Fat	1.0 g
Saturated Fat	0.3 g
Trans Fat	0.0 g
Cholesterol	110 mg
Sodium	220 mg
Potassium	390 mg
Total Carbohydrate	0 g
Dietary Fiber	0 g
Sugars	0 g
Protein	40 g
Phosphorus	295 mg

COOK'S TIP

If you use a zippered plastic bag to separate the grease, first pour the pan drippings into a 2-cup measuring cup, then into the bag. To remove the grease, hold the bag over a small glass bowl or saucepan, snip off a bottom corner of the bag, and allow the juice to run out, stopping when the grease is all that is left in the bag.

Hoisin Chicken

SERVES 4 ■ **SERVING SIZE** 3 ounces ■ **PREP TIME** 10 minutes ■ **COOK TIME** 8 minutes

3 tablespoons hoisin sauce

1 teaspoon orange zest

3 tablespoons orange juice

1 pound boneless, skinless chicken breasts, rinsed, patted dry, and cut into thin slices or strips

1. Stir the hoisin sauce, orange zest, and juice together in a small bowl and set aside.

2. Place a medium nonstick skillet over medium-high heat until hot. Coat the skillet with nonstick cooking spray, add the chicken, and cook 6–7 minutes or until the chicken just begins to lightly brown. Use two utensils to stir as you would when stir-frying.

3. Place the chicken on a serving platter. Add the hoisin mixture to the skillet and cook 15 seconds, stirring constantly. Spoon evenly over the chicken.

EXCHANGES / CHOICES

1/2 Carbohydrate
3 Protein, lean

Calories	160
Calories from Fat	25
Total Fat	3.0 g
Saturated Fat	0.8 g
Trans Fat	0.0 g
Cholesterol	65 mg
Sodium	260 mg
Potassium	230 mg
Total Carbohydrate	7 g
Dietary Fiber	0 g
Sugars	4 g
Protein	24 g
Phosphorus	180 mg

COOK'S TIP

For a striking contrast in color and flavor, serve on a bed of stir-fried snow peas or asparagus.

PORK

Sriracha-Roasted Pork with Sweet Potatoes

SERVES 4 ■ **SERVING SIZE** 3 ounces cooked pork and 3/4 cup potatoes
PREP TIME 10 minutes ■ **COOK TIME** 25 minutes

1 pound pork tenderloin

1 pound sweet potatoes, peeled and cut into 1-inch chunks (1/4 tsp salt and pepper)

2 tablespoons honey

1 tablespoon hot pepper sauce, such as sriracha

EXCHANGES / CHOICES

2 Starch
2 Protein, lean

Calories	280
Calories from Fat	50
Total Fat	5 g
Saturated Fat	1.4 g
Trans Fat	0.0 g
Cholesterol	75 mg
Sodium	310 mg
Potassium	985 mg
Total Carbohydrate	31 g
Dietary Fiber	6 g
Sugars	6 g
Protein	26 g
Phosphorus	340 mg

1 Preheat oven to 425°F.

2 Heat a large skillet coated with cooking spray over medium-high heat. Add the pork and brown on all sides, about 5 minutes total.

3 Place potatoes in a 13 × 9-inch baking pan. Coat potatoes with cooking spray and toss until well coated. Place the pork in the center of the potatoes and sprinkle 1/4 teaspoon salt and 1/4 teaspoon pepper evenly over all.

4 In a small bowl, combine the honey and sriracha sauce; set aside.

5 Bake 10 minutes, stir potatoes, spoon sauce over pork, and continue baking 15 minutes or until internal temperature of the pork reaches 150°F.

6 Place the pork on a cutting board and let stand 3 minutes before slicing. Meanwhile, gently toss the potatoes in the pan with any pan drippings. Cover to keep warm. Serve with pork.

Sriracha Roasted Pork
with Sweet Potatoes
page 105

Country-Style Ham and Potato Casserole

SERVES 4 ■ SERVING SIZE 1 1/2 cups ■ PREP TIME 15 minutes
BAKE TIME 40–45 minutes ■ STAND TIME 3 minutes

6 ounces lean smoked deli ham, (preferably Virginia ham), thinly sliced and chopped

1 pound red potatoes, scrubbed and thinly sliced

1 medium onion, thinly sliced

1/3 cup shredded, reduced-fat, sharp cheddar cheese

1. Preheat the oven to 350°F.

2. Place a medium nonstick skillet over medium-high heat until hot. Coat the skillet with nonstick cooking spray, add ham, and cook 5 minutes or until the ham edges are beginning to lightly brown, stirring frequently. Remove from the heat and set the ham aside on a separate plate.

3. Layer half of the potatoes and half of the onions in the bottom of the skillet. Top with the ham and repeat with layers of potatoes and onions. Sprinkle with black pepper, if desired, and cover tightly with a sheet of foil.

4. Bake 35–40 minutes or until the potatoes are tender when pierced with a fork. Remove from the oven, top with cheese, and let stand, uncovered, for 3 minutes to melt the cheese and develop flavors.

EXCHANGES / CHOICES

1 1/2 Starch
1 Protein, lean

Calories	170
Calories from Fat	20
Total Fat	2.5 g
Saturated Fat	1.2 g
Trans Fat	0.0 g
Cholesterol	25 mg
Sodium	420 mg
Potassium	660 mg
Total Carbohydrate	23 g
Dietary Fiber	2 g
Sugars	4 g
Protein	13 g
Phosphorus	205 mg

COOK'S TIP

Nonstick skillets will work fine in 350°F temperatures, even with plastic handles. You may cover the handle with foil, if you like. Or use a 12 × 8-inch glass baking dish (but you'll miss the flavor added by the skillet drippings).

Sausage Pilaf Peppers

SERVES 4 ■ **SERVING SIZE** 1 stuffed pepper ■ **PREP TIME** 8 minutes ■ **COOK TIME** 40 minutes

4 medium green bell peppers

6 ounces reduced-fat pork breakfast sausage

3/4 cup uncooked instant brown rice

2/3 cup salsa, divided use

1 Preheat the oven to 350°F.

2 Slice the tops off of each pepper and discard the seeds and membrane, leaving the peppers whole.

3 Coat a large nonstick skillet with nonstick cooking spray and place over medium-high heat until hot. Add the sausage and cook until it's no longer pink, breaking up large pieces while stirring.

4 Remove from the heat and add the rice and all but 1/4 cup salsa. Stir gently to blend.

5 Fill the peppers with equal amounts of the mixture and top each with 1 tablespoon salsa. Place the peppers in the skillet and cover tightly with foil. Bake 35 minutes or until the peppers are tender.

EXCHANGES / CHOICES

2 Starch
2 Nonstarchy Vegetable
1 Protein, medium fat

Calories	260
Calories from Fat	70
Total Fat	8.0 g
Saturated Fat	2.5 g
Trans Fat	0.1 g
Cholesterol	20 mg
Sodium	450 mg
Potassium	560 mg
Total Carbohydrate	37 g
Dietary Fiber	5 g
Sugars	5 g
Protein	11 g
Phosphorus	220 mg

COOK'S TIP

Nonstick skillets will work fine in 350°F, even with plastic handles. You may cover the handle with foil, if you like. Or use a small glass baking dish.

Anytime Skillet Pork

SERVES 4 ■ **SERVING SIZE** 1 chop ■ **PREP TIME** 5 minutes ■ **COOK TIME** 10 minutes

4 thin pork chops with bone in, trimmed of fat (about 1 1/4 pounds total)

1/3 cup water

1 1/2 teaspoons Worcestershire sauce

1 1/2 teaspoons lite soy sauce

1 Place a large nonstick skillet over medium-high heat until hot. Coat with nonstick cooking spray.

2 Liberally sprinkle the pork chops with pepper, if desired, and cook 3 minutes. Turn and cook 3 more minutes or until the pork is barely pink in the center. Set the pork aside on a separate plate and cover with foil to keep warm.

3 Stir the remaining ingredients together in a small bowl. Add the mixture to the skillet and bring to a boil over medium-high heat. Boil for 3–4 minutes or until the liquid is reduced to 2 tablespoons, stirring frequently. Spoon the sauce over the pork

EXCHANGES / CHOICES

3 Protein, lean

Calories	120
Calories from Fat	25
Total Fat	3.0 g
Saturated Fat	1.1 g
Trans Fat	0.0 g
Cholesterol	60 mg
Sodium	150 mg
Potassium	370 mg
Total Carbohydrate	1 g
Dietary Fiber	0 g
Sugars	0 g
Protein	22 g
Phosphorus	230 mg

COOK'S TIP

Try this for breakfast on a cold wintry day!

Pork with Tomato Caper Sauce

SERVES 4 ■ **SERVING SIZE** 1 chop ■ **PREP TIME** 10 minutes ■ **COOK TIME** 10 minutes

2 tablespoons tomato paste with oregano, basil, and garlic

2 tablespoons capers, drained and mashed with a fork

2/3 cup water, divided use

1/8 teaspoon salt

4 (4-ounce) boneless pork chops, trimmed of fat

1. Using a fork, stir the tomato paste, capers, and 1/3 cup water together in a small bowl.

2. Place a medium nonstick skillet over medium-high heat until hot. Coat the skillet with nonstick cooking spray, add the pork chops, and cook 3 minutes.

3. Turn the pork chops and immediately reduce the heat to medium. Spoon the tomato mixture evenly on top of each pork chop, cover tightly, and cook 5 minutes or until the pork chops are barely pink in the center. The sauce may be dark in some areas.

4. Remove the skillet from the heat and add the remaining 1/3 cup water and salt. Turn the pork chops over several times to remove the sauce. Place the pork chops on a serving plate and set aside.

5. Increase the heat to medium high. Bring the sauce to a boil, stirring constantly, and boil 1 minute or until the sauce begins to thicken slightly and measures 1/2 cup. Spoon the sauce over the pork chops.

EXCHANGES / CHOICES

3 Protein, lean

Calories	140
Calories from Fat	30
Total Fat	3.5 g
Saturated Fat	1.2 g
Trans Fat	0.0 g
Cholesterol	65 mg
Sodium	330 mg
Potassium	470 mg
Total Carbohydrate	2 g
Dietary Fiber	0 g
Sugars	1 g
Protein	25 g
Phosphorus	260 mg

COOK'S TIP

Don't overcook the pork chops in Step 3—they continue to cook while you finish the dish.

Pork with Pineapple Ginger Salsa

SERVES 4 ■ **SERVING SIZE** 1 chop plus 1/4 cup salsa ■ **PREP TIME** 10 minutes ■ **COOK TIME** 12 minutes

1 (8-ounce) can pineapple tidbits packed in juice, drained, reserve juice

2 teaspoons grated gingerroot

1/2–1 medium jalapeño, seeded and minced

1 teaspoon pourable sugar substitute (optional)

4 (4-ounce) boneless pork chops, trimmed of fat

1/4 teaspoon salt

1/4 teaspoon black pepper

1 Stir the pineapple, 1 tablespoon of the reserved pineapple juice, gingerroot, jalapeño, and 1 teaspoon sugar substitute (if desired), together in a small bowl and set aside.

2 Sprinkle both sides of the pork evenly with salt and pepper.

3 Place a large nonstick skillet over medium-high heat until hot. Coat the skillet with nonstick cooking spray, add the pork, and cook 4 minutes. Turn and cook 4 minutes longer or until the pork is barely pink in the center.

4 Add the remaining pineapple juice to the pork in the skillet and cook 2 minutes. Turn and cook 1 minute longer or until the liquid has evaporated. Remove the skillet from the heat, turn the pork several times to lightly glaze with the salsa, and serve.

EXCHANGES / CHOICES

1/2 Fruit
3 Protein, lean

Calories	170
Calories from Fat	30
Total Fat	3.5 g
Saturated Fat	1.2 g
Trans Fat	0.0 g
Cholesterol	65 mg
Sodium	210 mg
Potassium	490 mg
Total Carbohydrate	10 g
Dietary Fiber	1 g
Sugars	8 g
Protein	25 g
Phosphorus	260 mg

COOK'S TIP

If tidbits are not available, use pineapple chunks and cut them in smaller pieces.

Grapefruit-Zested Pork

SERVES 4 ■ **SERVING SIZE** 1 chop ■ **PREP TIME** 8 minutes
■ **MARINATE TIME** 8 hours ■ **COOK TIME** 6 minutes

3 tablespoons lite soy sauce

1/2–1 teaspoon grapefruit zest

3 tablespoons grapefruit juice

1 jalapeño pepper, seeded and finely chopped, or 1/8–1/4 teaspoon dried red pepper flakes

4 thin lean pork chops with bone in (about 1 1/4 pounds total)

1 Combine all ingredients in a large zippered plastic bag. Seal tightly and toss back and forth to coat evenly. Refrigerate overnight or at least 8 hours.

2 Preheat the broiler.

3 Coat the broiler rack and pan with nonstick cooking spray, arrange the pork chops on the rack (discarding the marinade), and broil 2 inches away from the heat source for 3 minutes. Turn and broil 3 minutes longer or until the pork is no longer pink in the center.

EXCHANGES / CHOICES

3 Protein, lean

Calories	130
Calories from Fat	25
Total Fat	3.0 g
Saturated Fat	1.1 g
Trans Fat	0.0 g
Cholesterol	60 mg
Sodium	270 mg
Potassium	390 mg
Total Carbohydrate	2 g
Dietary Fiber	0 g
Sugars	1 g
Protein	23 g
Phosphorus	235 mg

COOK'S TIP

You can marinate the pork up to 48 hours, if you like.

Sweet Sherry'd Pork Tenderloin

SERVES 4 ■ **SERVING SIZE** 3 ounces pork plus 2 tablespoons sauce ■ **PREP TIME** 4 minutes
MARINATE TIME 8 hours ■ **COOK TIME** 22 minutes ■ **STAND TIME** 3 minutes

1 pound pork tenderloin

1/4 cup dry sherry (divided use)

3 tablespoons lite soy sauce
(divided use)

1/3 cup peach all-fruit spread

1 Place the pork, 2 tablespoons sherry, and 2 tablespoons soy sauce in a quart-sized zippered plastic bag. Seal tightly and toss back and forth to coat evenly. Refrigerate overnight or at least 8 hours.

2 Stir the fruit spread, 2 tablespoons sherry, and 1 tablespoon soy sauce together in a small bowl. Cover with plastic wrap and refrigerate until needed.

3 Preheat the oven to 425°F.

4 Remove the pork from the marinade and discard the marinade. Place a medium nonstick skillet over medium-high heat until hot. Coat the skillet with nonstick cooking spray, add the pork, and brown on all sides.

5 Place the pork in a 9-inch pie pan and bake 15 minutes or until the pork is barely pink in the center. Place the pork on a cutting board and let stand 3 minutes before slicing.

6 Meanwhile, place the fruit spread mixture in the skillet and bring to a boil over medium-high heat, stirring frequently. Place the sauce on the bottom of a serving plate and arrange the pork on top. Sprinkle evenly with black pepper, if desired.

EXCHANGES / CHOICES

1 Carbohydrate
3 Protein, lean

Calories	190
Calories from Fat	25
Total Fat	3.0 g
Saturated Fat	1.0 g
Trans Fat	0.0 g
Cholesterol	60 mg
Sodium	320 mg
Potassium	400 mg
Total Carbohydrate	14 g
Dietary Fiber	0 g
Sugars	11 g
Protein	23 g
Phosphorus	210 mg

COOK'S TIP

You can marinate the pork up to 48 hours, if you like.

Sweet Jerk Pork

SERVES 4 ■ **SERVING SIZE** 3 ounces ■ **PREP TIME** 7 minutes ■ **MARINATE TIME** 15 minutes ■ **COOK TIME** 20 minutes ■ **STAND TIME** 25 minutes

1 pound pork tenderloin

2 teaspoons jerk seasoning

2 tablespoons packed dark brown sugar

2 teaspoons Worcestershire sauce

1 Preheat the oven to 425°F.

2 Sprinkle the pork evenly with the jerk seasoning and press down gently so the spices adhere. Let the pork stand 15 minutes.

3 Stir the sugar and Worcestershire sauce together in a small bowl until well blended. Coat an 11 × 7-inch baking pan with nonstick cooking spray and set aside.

4 Place a large nonstick skillet over medium-high heat until hot. Coat the skillet with nonstick cooking spray, add the pork, and brown all sides, about 5 minutes, turning occasionally.

5 Place the pork in the baking pan and spoon all but 1 tablespoon of the Worcestershire mixture evenly over the pork. Bake for 13–15 minutes or until the pork is barely pink in the center and a meat thermometer reaches 170°F.

6 Place the pork on a cutting board, spoon the remaining 1 tablespoon Worcestershire mixture evenly over all, and let stand 10 minutes before slicing.

EXCHANGES / CHOICES

1/2 Carbohydrate
3 Protein, lean

Calories	150
Calories from Fat	25
Total Fat	3.0 g
Saturated Fat	1.0 g
Trans Fat	0.0 g
Cholesterol	60 mg
Sodium	210 mg
Potassium	380 mg
Total Carbohydrate	8 g
Dietary Fiber	0 g
Sugars	8 g
Protein	22 g
Phosphorus	200 mg

COOK'S TIP

Since pork tenderloins are usually sold in 2-pound packages, 2 tenderloins to a package, use one in this recipe and wrap the other one in plastic wrap and freeze for another use.

Country-Style Ham and
Potato Casserole

page 107

Pork with Kalamata Rice

SERVES 4 ■ **SERVING SIZE** 3 ounces pork plus 1/2 cup rice
PREP TIME 9 minutes ■ **COOK TIME** 8 minutes

1/3 cup medium salsa

12 small kalamata olives, pitted and coarsely chopped

2 cups cooked brown rice, warm (omit added salt or fat)

4 (4-ounce) boneless pork chops, trimmed of fat

1/4 teaspoon salt

1/4 teaspoon black pepper

1/2 cup water

1. Add the salsa and olives to the cooked rice and toss gently. Place on a serving platter and cover with a sheet of foil to keep warm.

2. Place a large nonstick skillet over medium-high heat until hot. Coat the skillet with nonstick cooking spray. Sprinkle the pork with salt and pepper. Place the pork in the skillet, immediately reduce the heat to medium, and cook 4 minutes. Turn and cook 4 minutes longer or until the pork is barely pink in the center. Place the pork on top of the rice, cover with foil, and set aside.

3. Add the water to the skillet, stir, and bring to a boil over medium-high heat. Boil 2 minutes or until the liquid is reduced to 1/4 cup. Pour the sauce over the pork and rice.

EXCHANGES / CHOICES

1 1/2 Starch
3 Protein, lean

Calories	270
Calories from Fat	50
Total Fat	6.0 g
Saturated Fat	1.6 g
Trans Fat	0.0 g
Cholesterol	65 mg
Sodium	430 mg
Potassium	500 mg
Total Carbohydrate	24 g
Dietary Fiber	2 g
Sugars	1 g
Protein	28 g
Phosphorus	340 mg

COOK'S TIP

Adding the water to the pan drippings (a cooking technique called deglazing) in the last step pulls the flavors together while adding moisture to the dish.

Sizzling Pork Chops

SERVES 4 ■ **SERVING SIZE** 1 chop ■ **PREP TIME** 3 minutes
COOK TIME 12 minutes ■ **STAND TIME** 2 minutes

4 (4-ounce) boneless pork chops, trimmed of fat

1 tablespoon dried zesty Italian salad dressing and recipe mix (available in packets)

1 Coat both sides of the pork chops with the salad dressing mix, pressing down gently so the spices adhere.

2 Place a large nonstick skillet over medium heat until hot. Coat the skillet with nonstick cooking spray, add the pork, and cook 4 minutes. Turn and cook 4 minutes longer or until the pork is barely pink in the center.

3 Remove the skillet from the heat and let the pork stand in the skillet 2–3 minutes or until the pork begins to release some of its juices. Move the pork pieces around in the skillet several times to absorb the pan residue.

EXCHANGES / CHOICES

3 Protein, lean

Calories	140
Calories from Fat	30
Total Fat	3.5 g
Saturated Fat	1.2 g
Trans Fat	0.0 g
Cholesterol	65 mg
Sodium	390 mg
Potassium	390 mg
Total Carbohydrate	1 g
Dietary Fiber	0 g
Sugars	1 g
Protein	25 g
Phosphorus	255 mg

COOK'S TIP

Allowing the pork chops to stand briefly in the skillet, then moving them around in the pan, gives them a deep, dark color and rich flavor without adding other high-fat ingredients.

BEEF

Smoky Sirloin

SERVES 4 ■ **SERVING SIZE** 3 ounces cooked beef and 1 1/2 teaspoons sauce
PREP TIME 5 minutes ■ **COOK TIME** 12 minutes

1 pound boneless sirloin steak,
about 3/4-inch thick

1 1/2 teaspoons smoked paprika

2 tablespoons Worcestershire sauce

2 tablespoons balsamic vinegar

1 Sprinkle both sides of the beef with paprika,
1/4 teaspoon salt, and 1/4 teaspoon pepper. Press
down lightly to adhere. Let stand 15 minutes at room
temperature.

2 Heat a large skillet coated with cooking spray over
medium-high heat. Cook beef 4 to 5 minutes on each
side. Place on cutting board and let stand 5 minutes
before slicing.

3 Combine 1/4 cup water, Worcestershire sauce, and
vinegar. Pour into the skillet with any pan residue and
bring to a boil over medium-high heat. Boil 2 minutes
or until reduced to 2 tablespoons liquid. Pour over
sliced beef.

EXCHANGES / CHOICES

3 1/2 Protein, lean

Calories	150
Calories from Fat	30
Total Fat	3.0 g
Saturated Fat	1.0 g
Trans Fat	0 g
Cholesterol	70 mg
Sodium	280 mg
Potassium	500 mg
Total Carbohydrate	3 g
Dietary Fiber	0 g
Sugars	2 g
Protein	26 g
Phosphorus	295 mg

COOK'S TIP

For a slightly sweeter sauce, add 1/2 teaspoon sugar to the
Worcestershire sauce mixture before bringing to a boil.

Southwestern Protein-Powered Bowls

SERVES 4 ■ **SERVING SIZE** 1 cup ■ **PREP TIME** 5 minutes ■ **COOK TIME** 15 minutes

3/4 pound 90% extra-lean ground beef

1 (12.7-ounce) package frozen vegetable and grain protein blends, southwestern variety, such as Birds Eye Steam Fresh

1 (14.5-ounce) can no-salt-added diced tomatoes

1 tablespoon ground cumin

1 Heat a Dutch oven over medium-high heat. Add beef and cook until browned, stirring frequently. Stir in the frozen vegetable mixture, tomatoes, and 1 cup water. Bring to a boil. Reduce heat to medium-low, cover, and cook 10 minutes.

2 Remove from heat. Stir in the cumin, 1/4 teaspoon salt, and 1/4 teaspoon pepper, if desired.

3 Spoon equal amounts into 4 bowls.

EXCHANGES / CHOICES
1 1/2 Starch
1 Nonstarchy Vegetable
2 Protein, lean
1 Fat

Calories	280
Calories from Fat	80
Total Fat	9.0 g
Saturated Fat	3.0 g
Trans Fat	0.4 g
Cholesterol	50 mg
Sodium	450 mg
Potassium	650 mg
Total Carbohydrate	25 g
Dietary Fiber	8 g
Sugars	4 g
Protein	23 g
Phosphorus	235 mg

COOK'S TIP
For a slightly sweeter dish, add 1 teaspoon sugar with the cumin.

COOK'S TIP
Freezes well up to one month.

Homestyle Double-Onion Roast

SERVES 6 ■ **SERVING SIZE** 3 1/2 ounces beef plus 2/3 cup vegetables ■ **PREP TIME** 20 minutes
COOK TIME 1 hour and 10 minutes ■ **STAND TIME** 15 minutes

1 pound carrots, scrubbed, quartered lengthwise, and cut into 3-inch pieces

2 medium onions (8 ounces total), cut in 1/2-inch wedges and separated

1 3/4 pounds lean eye of round roast

1/4 cup water

2 1/2 tablespoons onion soup mix

1 Preheat the oven to 325°F.

2 Coat a 13 × 9-inch nonstick baking pan with nonstick cooking spray, arrange the carrots and onions in the pan, and set aside.

3 Place a medium nonstick skillet over medium-high heat until hot. Coat the skillet with nonstick cooking spray, add the beef, and brown 2 minutes. Turn and brown another 2 minutes.

4 Place the beef in the center of the baking pan on top of the vegetables. Add the water to the skillet and scrap up the pan drippings, then pour them over the beef. Sprinkle evenly with the soup mix.

5 Cover the pan tightly with foil and cook 1 hour and 5 minutes or until a meat thermometer reaches 135°F. Place the beef on a cutting board and let stand 15 minutes before slicing. (The temperature will rise another 10°F while the beef stands.)

6 Keep the vegetables in the pan covered to keep warm. Place the beef slices on a serving platter, arrange the vegetables around the beef, and spoon the pan liquids evenly over the beef.

EXCHANGES / CHOICES

2 Nonstarchy Vegetable
4 Protein, lean

Calories	220
Calories from Fat	40
Total Fat	4.5 g
Saturated Fat	1.5 g
Trans Fat	0.0 g
Cholesterol	60 mg
Sodium	410 mg
Potassium	540 mg
Total Carbohydrate	13 g
Dietary Fiber	3 g
Sugars	5 g
Protein	32 g
Phosphorus	240 mg

COOK'S TIP

These leftovers freeze well for later use.

Simply Seared Beef Tenderloin

SERVES 4 ■ SERVING SIZE 1 tenderloin and 1/2 cup rice
PREP TIME 3 minutes ■ COOK TIME 11 minutes

4 (5-ounce) beef tenderloin steaks, about 3/4-inch thick, trimmed of fat

1 large split garlic clove

1/4 teaspoon coarsely ground black pepper

1/4 teaspoon salt

2 teaspoons Worcestershire sauce

1/2 teaspoon beef bouillon granules

1/2 cup water

2 cups cooked wild rice

1 Rub the beef with the garlic clove. Place a large nonstick skillet over medium-high heat until hot. Coat the skillet with nonstick cooking spray, add the beef, and cook 3 minutes. Turn and cook another 2 minutes.

2 Reduce the heat to medium low and cook the steaks 4 minutes longer or until they are done as desired, turning once. Set aside on a separate plate.

3 Increase the heat to medium high, add the remaining ingredients, bring to a boil, and continue boiling 1 minute or until the mixture measures 1/4 cup liquid. Pour the juices over the beef. Serve each tenderloin with 1/2 cup wild rice.

EXCHANGES / CHOICES

1 Starch
4 Protein, lean

Calories	260
Calories from Fat	70
Total Fat	8.0 g
Saturated Fat	2.8 g
Trans Fat	0.0 g
Cholesterol	75 mg
Sodium	340 mg
Potassium	440 mg
Total Carbohydrate	19 g
Dietary Fiber	2 g
Sugars	1 g
Protein	29 g
Phosphorus	280 mg

COOK'S TIP

You can also prepare this beef with 1/2 cup strong coffee instead of the bouillon granules and water—you'll find the coffee intensifies the hearty beef flavor.

Beef Strips
with Sweet Ginger Sauce

SERVES 4 ■ **SERVING SIZE** 1/2 cup ■ **PREP TIME** 4 minutes ■ **COOK TIME** 4 minutes

2 tablespoons lite soy sauce

1 tablespoon sugar

2 teaspoons grated gingerroot

1 pound boneless top round or
   sirloin steak, trimmed of fat and
   sliced into strips

1 Stir the soy sauce, sugar, and gingerroot together in a
   small bowl and set aside.

2 Place a large nonstick skillet over medium-high
   heat until hot. Coat the skillet with nonstick cooking
   spray, add half the beef, and cook 1 minute, stirring
   constantly.

3 Remove the beef from the skillet and set aside on
   a separate plate. Recoat the skillet with nonstick
   cooking spray and cook the remaining beef 1 minute.

4 Return the first batch of beef to the skillet, add the soy
   sauce mixture, and cook 1 minute to heat thoroughly.

EXCHANGES / CHOICES

3 Protein, lean

Calories	150
Calories from Fat	30
Total Fat	3.5 g
Saturated Fat	1.1 g
Trans Fat	0.0 g
Cholesterol	60 mg
Sodium	300 mg
Potassium	240 mg
Total Carbohydrate	4 g
Dietary Fiber	0 g
Sugars	3 g
Protein	24 g
Phosphorus	155 mg

COOK'S TIP

To grate fresh gingerroot, first peel off the outer skin with a
sharp knife and use a fine grater for best results.

Sirloin Hoagies

SERVES 4 ■ **SERVING SIZE** 1 hoagie ■ **PREP TIME** 12 minutes ■ **COOK TIME** 16 minutes

1/8 teaspoon salt (divided use)

1/2 teaspoon black pepper

1 pound boneless sirloin steak, trimmed of fat

1 large onion, thinly sliced (about 1 1/2 cups)

1/2 cup water

8 ounces whole-wheat or white French bread

1 1/2 tablespoons prepared mustard

1 Preheat the oven to 350°F.

2 Sprinkle 1/16 teaspoon salt and the pepper evenly over both sides of the steak. Place a large nonstick skillet over medium-high heat until hot. Coat with nonstick cooking spray, add the steak, and cook 5 minutes.

3 Turn and cook another 4 minutes or until the beef is done as desired. Place the beef on a cutting board and set aside.

4 Coat the pan drippings with nonstick cooking spray, reduce the heat to medium, and add the onions. Coat the onions with nonstick cooking spray and cook 6–7 minutes or until they are richly browned, stirring frequently.

5 Add water to the onions and cook 1 minute or until most of the moisture has evaporated, stirring constantly. Remove from heat.

6 Wrap the bread in foil, place in the oven, and bake 5 minutes or until hot. Meanwhile, thinly slice the beef diagonally.

7 Using a serrated knife, cut the bread in half lengthwise and spread a thin layer of mustard on each side. Top with beef, then onions and any juices. Sprinkle with the remaining salt, top with the other bread half, and cut in fourths crosswise.

EXCHANGES / CHOICES

2 Starch
1 Nonstarchy Vegetable
3 Protein, lean

Calories	290
Calories from Fat	45
Total Fat	5.0 g
Saturated Fat	1.6 g
Trans Fat	0.1 g
Cholesterol	40 mg
Sodium	400 mg
Potassium	450 mg
Total Carbohydrate	32 g
Dietary Fiber	3 g
Sugars	2 g
Protein	28 g
Phosphorus	285 mg

COOK'S TIP

When buying boneless beef or pork for a recipe asking you to trim the fat, purchase about 4 ounces more than the recipe calls for. For example, 1 1/4 pounds boneless beef or pork will yield 1 pound meat after you trim the fat.

Zesty Beef Patties with Grilled Onions

SERVES 4 ■ **SERVING SIZE** 1 patty plus 1/4 cup onions ■ **PREP TIME** 7 minutes ■ **COOK TIME** 15 minutes

1 pound 96% lean ground beef

1 tablespoon Dijon mustard

4 teaspoons ranch-style salad dressing and seasoning mix (available in packets)

1 large yellow onion, thinly sliced

1/4 cup water

1. Mix the ground beef, mustard, and salad dressing mix together in a medium bowl. Shape the beef mixture into 4 patties.

2. Place a large nonstick skillet over medium-high heat until hot. Coat the skillet with nonstick cooking spray and add the onions. Coat the onions with nonstick cooking spray and cook 7 minutes or until they are richly browned, stirring frequently. Set them aside on a separate plate.

3. Recoat the skillet with nonstick cooking spray, add the patties, and cook 4 minutes. Flip the patties and cook another 3 minutes or until they are no longer pink in the center. Place them on a serving platter.

4. Add the onions and water to the pan drippings and cook 30 seconds, scraping the bottom and sides of the skillet. When the mixture has thickened slightly, spoon it over the patties.

EXCHANGES / CHOICES

1 Nonstarchy Vegetable
4 Protein, lean

Calories	190
Calories from Fat	45
Total Fat	5.0 g
Saturated Fat	2.2 g
Trans Fat	0.3 g
Cholesterol	65 mg
Sodium	450 mg
Potassium	490 mg
Total Carbohydrate	8 g
Dietary Fiber	1 g
Sugars	3 g
Protein	26 g
Phosphorus	245 mg

COOK'S TIP

Be sure to use the dry seasoning mix in this recipe, not the liquid ranch dressing.

Cumin'd Beef Patties and Santa Fe Sour Cream

SERVES 4 ■ **SERVING SIZE** 1 patty plus 1 1/2 tablespoons sour cream
PREP TIME 5 minutes ■ **COOK TIME** 8 minutes

1 pound 96% lean ground beef

1/3 cup mild picante sauce (divided use)

2 teaspoons ground cumin

1/8 teaspoon salt (divided use)

1/8 teaspoon black pepper

1/4 cup fat-free sour cream

2 whole-wheat hamburger buns

1. Mix the ground beef, all but 2 tablespoons of the picante sauce, cumin, 1/16 teaspoon salt, and black pepper in a medium bowl until well blended. Shape the beef mixture into 4 patties.

2. Place a large nonstick skillet over medium-high heat until hot. Coat the skillet with nonstick cooking spray, add the patties, and cook 4 minutes. Flip the patties and cook another 3 minutes or until they are no longer pink in the center.

3. Meanwhile, stir 2 tablespoons picante sauce, 1/16 teaspoon salt, and the sour cream together in a small bowl.

4. Serve each patty on 1/2 of a hamburger bun and top with 1 1/2 tablespoons sour cream. Spoon an additional 1/2 teaspoon picante sauce on top of each serving, if desired.

EXCHANGES / CHOICES

1 Starch
3 Protein, lean

Calories	230
Calories from Fat	50
Total Fat	6.0 g
Saturated Fat	2.4 g
Trans Fat	0.3 g
Cholesterol	65 mg
Sodium	460 mg
Potassium	540 mg
Total Carbohydrate	15 g
Dietary Fiber	2 g
Sugars	3 g
Protein	29 g
Phosphorus	300 mg

COOK'S TIP

Picante sauce is a bit thinner than salsa, but the two can be used interchangeably in most recipes.

Sirloin Hoagies
page 124

Chili-Stuffed Potatoes

SERVES 4 ■ **SERVING SIZE** 1 potato stuffed with 1/2 cup chili
PREP TIME 5 minutes ■ **COOK TIME** 10 minutes

4 (8-ounce) baking potatoes, preferably Yukon Gold, scrubbed and pierced several times with a fork

12 ounces 90% lean ground beef

3/4 cup water

1 (1.25-ounce) packet chili seasoning mix

1 Microwave the potatoes on HIGH 10–11 minutes or until they are tender when pierced with a fork.

2 Meanwhile, place a large nonstick skillet over medium-high heat until hot. Coat the skillet with nonstick cooking spray, add the beef, and cook until the beef is no longer pink, stirring frequently.

3 Add the water and chili seasoning and stir. Cook 1–2 minutes or until thickened.

4 Split the potatoes almost in half and fluff with a fork. Spoon 1/2 cup chili onto each potato and top with sour cream or cheese (if desired).

EXCHANGES / CHOICES

3 Starch
2 Protein, lean

Calories	350
Calories from Fat	70
Total Fat	8.0 g
Saturated Fat	2.8 g
Trans Fat	0.4 g
Cholesterol	50 mg
Sodium	410 mg
Potassium	1180 mg
Total Carbohydrate	48 g
Dietary Fiber	5 g
Sugars	3 g
Protein	21 g
Phosphorus	335 mg

COOK'S TIP

It's important to pierce the potatoes several times in different areas before microwaving them. This allows the built-up steam to be released and the potatoes to cook more quickly.

Bourbon'd Filet Mignon

SERVES 4 ■ **SERVING SIZE** 1 steak plus 1/3 cup wild rice ■ **PREP TIME** 5 minutes
MARINATE TIME 15 minutes ■ **COOK TIME** 8–12 minutes

1/2 teaspoon salt (divided use)

1/8–1/4 teaspoon coarsely ground
black pepper

4 5-ounce filet mignon steaks
(or beef tenderloin), about
3/4-inch thick, trimmed of fat

1/2 cup strong coffee (or 1/2 cup water
and 1 teaspoon instant coffee granules)

2 tablespoons bourbon

2 teaspoons Worcestershire sauce

1 1/3 cups cooked wild rice

1. Sprinkle 1/4 teaspoon salt and the black pepper evenly over both sides of the beef and let stand 15 minutes. Preheat the oven to 200°F.

2. Meanwhile, stir the coffee, bourbon, Worcestershire sauce, and 1/4 teaspoon salt together in a small bowl.

3. Place a large nonstick skillet over high heat until hot. Coat the skillet with nonstick cooking spray, add the steaks, and cook 3 minutes on each side.

4. Reduce the heat to medium low and cook the steaks 2–6 minutes longer or until they are done as desired. Place them on individual dinner plates in the oven.

5. Add the coffee mixture to the skillet, bring to a boil over high heat, and boil 2 minutes or until the liquid is reduced to 2 tablespoons. Spoon the sauce evenly over beef and serve immediately over cooked wild rice.

EXCHANGES / CHOICES

1 Starch
4 Protein, lean

Calories	250
Calories from Fat	60
Total Fat	7.0 g
Saturated Fat	2.8 g
Trans Fat	0.0 g
Cholesterol	75 mg
Sodium	370 mg
Potassium	420 mg
Total Carbohydrate	12 g
Dietary Fiber	1 g
Sugars	1 g
Protein	28 g
Phosphorus	255 mg

COOK'S TIP

There's no need to heat the water before combining it with the instant coffee granules. The granules dissolve just fine in cold water.

Stewed Beef and Ale

SERVES 4 ■ **SERVING SIZE** 3/4 cup ■ **PREP TIME** 15 minutes ■ **COOK TIME** 1 hour and 40 minutes

1 pound boneless top round steak,
   cut in 1/4 inch × 3 1/2-inch strips

1 cup chopped onion

1 (14.5-ounce) can stewed tomatoes

1 cup beer

1 teaspoon sugar (optional)

1/4 teaspoon salt

1/4 teaspoon black pepper

1. Place a large nonstick skillet over medium-high heat until hot. Coat the skillet with nonstick cooking spray. Working in two batches, add half of the beef strips and brown, stirring constantly, and set aside on a separate plate. Repeat with the remaining beef strips.

2. Recoat the skillet with nonstick cooking spray, add the onions, and cook 4 minutes or until the onions are translucent, stirring frequently. Add the remaining ingredients, including the beef and any accumulated juices.

3. Bring to a boil over high heat, then reduce the heat, cover tightly, and simmer 1 hour and 30 minutes or until the beef is very tender. Using the back of a spoon, mash the beef pieces to thicken the dish slightly.

EXCHANGES / CHOICES

2 Nonstarchy Vegetable
3 Protein, lean

Calories	180
Calories from Fat	30
Total Fat	3.5 g
Saturated Fat	1.2 g
Trans Fat	0.0 g
Cholesterol	60 mg
Sodium	390 mg
Potassium	490 mg
Total Carbohydrate	10 g
Dietary Fiber	2 g
Sugars	7 g
Protein	25 g
Phosphorus	180 mg

COOK'S TIP

You probably don't want to omit the sugar in this recipe—it offsets the beer and calms down the acidity of the tomatoes (even though they are the stewed variety, already a little sweeter than other canned tomatoes).

Extra-Easy Meatballs

SERVES 6 ■ **SERVING SIZE** 2/3 cup (4 meatballs plus sauce)
PREP TIME 15 minutes ■ **COOK TIME** 30 minutes

1 pound 95% lean ground beef

1/2 cup quick-cooking oats

3 large egg whites

1 (25.5-ounce) jar meatless, fat-free, low-sodium spaghetti sauce (divided use)

1/4 teaspoon salt

1 Mix the ground beef, oats, egg whites, 1/2 cup spaghetti sauce, and salt together in a large bowl. (You can also add 1 tablespoon dried basil, if desired.) Shape the mixture into 24 (1-inch) meatballs.

2 Place a large nonstick skillet over medium-high heat until hot. Coat with nonstick cooking spray, add the meatballs, and cook until browned, stirring frequently. Use two utensils to stir as you would when stir-frying.

3 Add the remaining spaghetti sauce and bring just to a boil. Reduce the heat, cover tightly, and simmer 20 minutes.

EXCHANGES / CHOICES

1 Starch
2 Protein, lean

Calories	170
Calories from Fat	35
Total Fat	4.0 g
Saturated Fat	1.6 g
Trans Fat	0.1 g
Cholesterol	45 mg
Sodium	180 mg
Potassium	620 mg
Total Carbohydrate	13 g
Dietary Fiber	1 g
Sugars	7 g
Protein	19 g
Phosphorus	195 mg

COOK'S TIP

This recipe makes a great meatball sandwich.

Tender Green Pepper'd Top Round

SERVES 4 ■ **SERVING SIZE** 1/4 recipe ■ **PREP TIME** 10 minutes
MARINATE TIME 8 hours ■ **COOK TIME** 60 minutes

1 pound boneless top round steak,
    trimmed of fat and cut in 4 equal pieces

1/4 cup fat-free Italian salad dressing

1 cup water

1/4 cup ketchup

1/4 teaspoon salt

1/4 teaspoon black pepper

2 medium green bell peppers,
    cut in thin strips

1 Place the beef and salad dressing in a large zippered plastic bag. Seal tightly and shake back and forth to coat evenly. Refrigerate overnight or at least 8 hours, turning occasionally.

2 Stir the water, ketchup, salt, and black pepper together in a small bowl and set aside.

3 Place a large nonstick skillet over medium-high heat until hot. Coat the skillet with nonstick cooking spray. Remove the beef from the marinade, discard the marinade, and place the steaks in the skillet. Cook 3 minutes, then turn and cook another 2 minutes.

4 Reduce the heat to medium low and cook the steaks 4 minutes longer or until they are done as desired, turning once. Add the green peppers and pour the ketchup mixture over all. Bring to a boil, reduce the heat, cover tightly, and simmer 55 minutes or until very tender.

EXCHANGES / CHOICES

1/2 Carbohydrate
3 Protein, lean

Calories	160
Calories from Fat	30
Total Fat	3.5 g
Saturated Fat	1.2 g
Trans Fat	0.0 g
Cholesterol	60 mg
Sodium	430 mg
Potassium	420 mg
Total Carbohydrate	8 g
Dietary Fiber	1 g
Sugars	6 g
Protein	25 g
Phosphorus	175 mg

COOK'S TIP

Here's a great time saver: buy an extra pound of steak, place it in a zippered plastic bag with 1/4 cup Italian salad dressing, and freeze it for a later use. It will marinate while freezing and defrosting, and you can have flavorful meat in a flash!

Spicy Chili'd Sirloin Steak

SERVES 4 ■ **SERVING SIZE** 3 ounces ■ **PREP TIME** 2 minutes ■ **MARINATE TIME** 15 minutes
COOK TIME 11 minutes ■ **STAND TIME** 2 minutes

1 pound boneless sirloin steak, trimmed of fat

2 tablespoons chili seasoning (available in packets)

1/8 teaspoon salt

1. Coat both sides of the sirloin with the chili seasoning mix, pressing down so the spices adhere. Let stand 15 minutes, or overnight in the refrigerator for a spicier flavor (let steak stand at room temperature 15 minutes before cooking).

2. Place a large nonstick skillet over medium-high heat until hot. Coat the skillet with nonstick cooking spray, add the beef, and cook 5 minutes. Turn the steak, reduce the heat to medium, cover tightly, and cook 5 minutes. Do not overcook. Remove the skillet from the heat and let stand 2 minutes, covered.

3. Sprinkle the steak with salt and cut into 1/4-inch slices. Pour any accumulated juices over the steak slices.

EXCHANGES / CHOICES

3 Protein, lean

Calories	140
Calories from Fat	40
Total Fat	4.5 g
Saturated Fat	1.6 g
Trans Fat	0.1 g
Cholesterol	40 mg
Sodium	250 mg
Potassium	340 mg
Total Carbohydrate	2 g
Dietary Fiber	0 g
Sugars	0 g
Protein	23 g
Phosphorus	180 mg

COOK'S TIP

Cook the steak quickly at a higher temperature. Reduce the heat and cover the skillet, searing the delicious meat juices without drying out the meat.

SEAFOOD

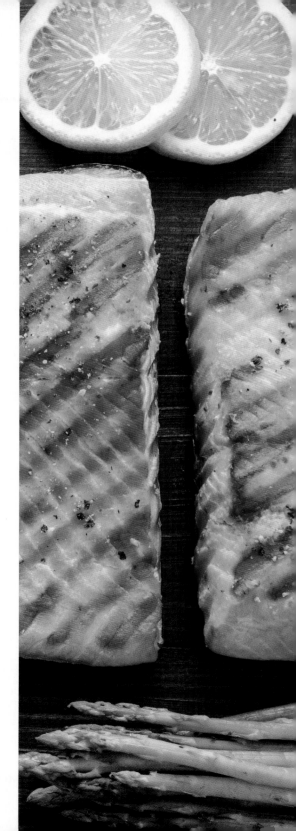

Buttery Lemon Grilled Fish on Grilled Asparagus

SERVES 4 ■ **SERVING SIZE** 3 ounces cooked fish; 6–8 asparagus spears; and 1 tablespoon topping
PREP TIME 5 minutes ■ **COOK TIME** 12 minutes

1 pound asparagus spears, ends trimmed

4 (4-ounce) cod filets, rinsed and patted dry

Juice and zest of a medium lemon

1/4 cup light butter with canola oil

1. Heat a grill or grill pan over medium-high heat. Coat the asparagus with cooking spray and cook 6–8 minutes or until just tender-crisp, turning occasionally. Set aside on a rimmed serving platter and cover to keep warm.

2. Coat both sides of the fish with cooking spray, sprinkle with 1/4 teaspoon black pepper, if desired, and cook 3 minutes on each side or until opaque in center.

3. Meanwhile, combine the light butter, lemon zest and 1/4 teaspoon salt, if desired, in a small bowl.

4. Spoon the butter mixture over the asparagus and spread over all. Top with the fish and squeeze lemon juice over fish.

EXCHANGES / CHOICES

1 Nonstarchy Vegetable
3 Protein, lean
1/2 Fat

Calories	160
Calories from Fat	60
Total Fat	6.0 g
Saturated Fat	1.4 g
Trans Fat	0.0 g
Cholesterol	50 mg
Sodium	210 mg
Potassium	635 mg
Total Carbohydrate	6 g
Dietary Fiber	3 g
Sugars	3 g
Protein	23 g
Phosphorus	265 mg

Shrimp and Noodles Parmesan

SERVES 4 ■ **SERVING SIZE** 1 1/2 cups ■ **PREP TIME** 2 minutes ■ **COOK TIME** 10 minutes

8 ounces uncooked whole-wheat no-yolk egg noodles

1 pound peeled raw shrimp, rinsed and patted dry

1/4 cup no-trans-fat margarine (35% vegetable oil)

1/4 teaspoon salt

3 tablespoons grated fresh Parmesan cheese

1. Cook noodles according to package directions, omitting any salt or fat.

2. Meanwhile, place a large nonstick skillet over medium heat until hot. Coat with nonstick cooking spray and sauté the shrimp for 4–5 minutes or until opaque in the center, stirring frequently.

3. Drain the noodles well in a colander and place in a pasta bowl. Add the margarine, shrimp, salt, and black pepper, to taste (if desired), and toss gently. Sprinkle evenly with the Parmesan cheese.

EXCHANGES CHOICES

3 Starch
3 Protein, lean

Calories	340
Calories from Fat	60
Total Fat	7.0 g
Saturated Fat	1.9 g
Trans Fat	0.0 g
Cholesterol	190 mg
Sodium	410 mg
Potassium	390 mg
Total Carbohydrate	42 g
Dietary Fiber	6 g
Sugars	0 g
Protein	33 g
Phosphorus	410 mg

COOK'S TIP

If you buy frozen shrimp, place it in a colander and run under cold water until the shrimp are partially thawed, about 1 minute.

Lemon-Peppered Shrimp

SERVES 4 ■ **SERVING SIZE** 1/2 cup ■ **PREP TIME** 2 minutes ■ **COOK TIME** 7 minutes

1 pound peeled raw shrimp, rinsed and patted dry

1 tablespoon salt-free steak seasoning blend

1 teaspoon lemon zest

2–3 tablespoons lemon juice

3 tablespoons no-trans-fat margarine (35% vegetable oil)

1/4 teaspoon salt

1 Place a large nonstick skillet over medium heat until hot. Coat the skillet with nonstick cooking spray, add the shrimp, sprinkle evenly with the steak seasoning, and cook 5 minutes or until the shrimp is opaque in the center, stirring frequently.

2 Stir in the lemon zest, juice, margarine, and salt and cook 1 minute.

EXCHANGES / CHOICES
3 Protein, lean

Calories	140
Calories from Fat	35
Total Fat	4.0 g
Saturated Fat	0.9 g
Trans Fat	0.0 g
Cholesterol	190 mg
Sodium	320 mg
Potassium	280 mg
Total Carbohydrate	2 g
Dietary Fiber	1 g
Sugars	0 g
Protein	24 g
Phosphorus	240 mg

COOK'S TIP
Serve this in individual au gratin dishes or over steamed rice.

Buttery Lemon Grilled
Fish on Grilled Asparagus
page 135

Tilapia with Caper'd Sour Cream

SERVES 4 ■ **SERVING SIZE** 1 filet plus 1 tablespoon sour cream
PREP TIME 6 minutes ■ **COOK TIME** 6 minutes

1 tablespoon capers, drained

1/4 teaspoon salt (divided use)

1/4 cup reduced-fat sour cream

4 (4-ounce) tilapia filets, rinsed and patted dry

1/4 teaspoon black pepper

1 medium lemon, quartered

1. Mash the capers with a fork or the back of a spoon. Stir the capers and 1/8 teaspoon salt into the sour cream.

2. Place a large nonstick skillet over medium heat until hot. Coat the skillet with nonstick cooking spray. Sprinkle one side of each filet evenly with the black pepper and 1/8 teaspoon salt. Cook 3 minutes, then turn and cook 2–3 minutes longer or until the fish is opaque in the center.

3. Place the filets on a serving platter, squeeze lemon juice evenly over all, and top each filet with 1 tablespoon sour cream.

EXCHANGES / CHOICES
3 Protein, lean

Calories	130
Calories from Fat	20
Total Fat	2.5 g
Saturated Fat	0.9 g
Trans Fat	0.0 g
Cholesterol	50 mg
Sodium	270 mg
Potassium	360 mg
Total Carbohydrate	3 g
Dietary Fiber	0 g
Sugars	1 g
Protein	23 g
Phosphorus	190 mg

COOK'S TIP
Mash the capers extremely well for peak flavors.

Two-Sauce Cajun Fish

SERVES 4 ■ **SERVING SIZE** 1 filet ■ **PREP TIME** 10 minutes ■ **COOK TIME** 12–15 minutes

4 (4-ounce) tilapia filets (or any mild, lean white fish filets), rinsed and patted dry

1/2 teaspoon seafood seasoning

1 (14.5-ounce) can stewed tomatoes with Cajun seasonings, well drained

2 tablespoons no-trans-fat margarine (35% vegetable oil)

1 Preheat the oven to 400°F.

2 Coat a broiler rack and pan with nonstick cooking spray, arrange the fish filets on the rack about 2 inches apart, and sprinkle them evenly with the seafood seasoning.

3 Place the tomatoes in a blender and puree until just smooth. Set aside 1/4 cup of the mixture in a small glass bowl.

4 Spoon the remaining tomatoes evenly over the top of each filet and bake 12–15 minutes or until the filets are opaque in the center.

5 Meanwhile, add the margarine to the reserved 1/4 cup tomato mixture and microwave on HIGH 20 seconds or until the mixture is just melted. Stir to blend well.

6 Place the filets on a serving platter, spoon the tomato-margarine mixture over the center of each filet, and sprinkle each lightly with chopped fresh parsley, if desired.

EXCHANGES / CHOICES

3 Protein, lean

Calories	150
Calories from Fat	45
Total Fat	5.0 g
Saturated Fat	1.4 g
Trans Fat	0.0 g
Cholesterol	50 mg
Sodium	250 mg
Potassium	450 mg
Total Carbohydrate	4 g
Dietary Fiber	1 g
Sugars	3 g
Protein	23 g
Phosphorus	185 mg

COOK'S TIP

The filets are cooked on a broiler rack to keep any excess liquid from seeping into the tomatoes and making them too watery. The tomatoes cook just fine on top of the fish!

No-Fry Fish Fry

SERVES 4 ■ **SERVING SIZE** 1 filet ■ **PREP TIME** 7 minutes ■ **COOK TIME** 6 minutes

2 tablespoons yellow cornmeal

2 teaspoons Cajun seasoning

4 (4-ounce) tilapia filets (or any mild, lean white fish filets), rinsed and patted dry

1/8 teaspoon salt

Lemon wedges (optional)

1 Preheat the broiler.

2 Coat a broiler rack and pan with nonstick cooking spray and set aside.

3 Mix the cornmeal and Cajun seasoning thoroughly in a shallow pan, such as a pie plate. Coat each filet with nonstick cooking spray and coat evenly with the cornmeal mixture.

4 Place the filets on the rack and broil 6 inches away from the heat source for 3 minutes on each side.

5 Place the filets on a serving platter, sprinkle each evenly with salt, and serve with lemon wedges, if desired.

EXCHANGES / CHOICES

3 Protein, lean

Calories	130
Calories from Fat	20
Total Fat	2.5 g
Saturated Fat	0.8 g
Trans Fat	0.0 g
Cholesterol	50 mg
Sodium	250 mg
Potassium	360 mg
Total Carbohydrate	4 g
Dietary Fiber	0 g
Sugars	0 g
Protein	23 g
Phosphorus	185 mg

COOK'S TIP

Serve this dish immediately after you prepare it for peak flavor and texture.

Red Snapper with Fresh Tomato-Basil Sauce

SERVES 4 ■ **SERVING SIZE** 1 filet plus 1/2 cup sauce
PREP TIME 8 minutes ■ **COOK TIME** 12–15 minutes

4 (4-ounce) snapper filets (or any mild, lean white fish filets), rinsed and patted dry

1/4 teaspoon salt (divided use)

1/8 teaspoon black pepper

1 pint grape tomatoes, quartered (2 cups total)

2 tablespoons chopped fresh basil

2 ounces crumbled, reduced-fat, sun-dried tomato and basil feta cheese

1. Preheat the oven to 400°F.

2. Line a baking sheet with foil and coat with nonstick cooking spray. Arrange the filets on the foil about 2 inches apart. Sprinkle them evenly with 1/4 teaspoon salt and the pepper. Bake 12–15 minutes or until the filets are opaque in the center.

3. Combine the tomatoes, basil, and 1/4 teaspoon salt in a small saucepan. Cook over medium-high heat for 2 minutes or until the tomatoes are limp.

4. Place the filets on a serving platter, spoon the tomatoes evenly over the filets, and sprinkle each with feta.

EXCHANGES / CHOICES

1 Nonstarchy Vegetable
3 Protein, lean

Calories	160
Calories from Fat	40
Total Fat	4.5 g
Saturated Fat	2.1 g
Trans Fat	0.0 g
Cholesterol	50 mg
Sodium	360 mg
Potassium	690 mg
Total Carbohydrate	5 g
Dietary Fiber	2 g
Sugars	2 g
Protein	27 g
Phosphorus	250 mg

COOK'S TIP
Lining the baking sheet with foil makes for an easy cleanup!

Flounder with Zesty Cucumber Topping

SERVES 4 ■ **SERVING SIZE** 1 filet plus 1 1/2 tablespoons sauce
PREP TIME 7 minutes ■ **COOK TIME** 12–15 minutes

4 (4-ounce) flounder filets (or any mild, lean white fish filets), rinsed and patted dry

1/4 teaspoon black pepper

1/2 medium cucumber, peeled, seeded, and finely chopped

2 tablespoons reduced-fat mayonnaise

1/2 teaspoon lime zest

1 tablespoon lime juice

1/4 teaspoon salt

1 Preheat the oven to 400°F.

2 Line a baking sheet with foil and coat with nonstick cooking spray. Arrange the filets on the foil about 2 inches apart. Coat the filets with nonstick cooking spray, sprinkle them evenly with pepper, and bake 12–15 minutes or until the filets are opaque in the center.

3 Meanwhile, stir the mayonnaise, lime zest, juice, and salt together in a small bowl until well blended.

4 Place the filets on a serving platter, spoon sauce over the center of each, and serve with extra lime wedges alongside, if desired.

EXCHANGES / CHOICES

3 Protein, lean

Calories	130
Calories from Fat	25
Total Fat	3.0 g
Saturated Fat	0.6 g
Trans Fat	0.0 g
Cholesterol	60 mg
Sodium	300 mg
Potassium	340 mg
Total Carbohydrate	2 g
Dietary Fiber	0 g
Sugars	1 g
Protein	21 g
Phosphorus	260 mg

COOK'S TIP
Coating the filets with nonstick cooking spray keeps them moist while baking—without many calories from extra oil!

Shrimp and Sausage Rice

SERVES 4 ■ **SERVING SIZE** 1 cup ■ **PREP TIME** 10 minutes
COOK TIME 23 minutes ■ **STAND TIME** 5 minutes

4 ounces reduced-fat pork breakfast sausage

16 ounces frozen pepper stir-fry, thawed

1 1/4 cups water

3/4 cup instant brown rice

12 ounces peeled raw shrimp, rinsed and patted dry

1/4 teaspoon salt

1/4 teaspoon black pepper

1. Place a large nonstick skillet over medium-high heat until hot. Coat the skillet with nonstick cooking spray, add the sausage, and cook until browned, breaking up large pieces while cooking. Set the sausage aside to drain on paper towels.

2. Recoat the skillet with nonstick cooking spray, add the pepper stir-fry mixture, increase the heat to high, and cook 3 minutes or until most of the liquid has evaporated.

3. Add the water and bring to a boil. Reduce the heat, cover tightly, and simmer 10 minutes or until vegetables are tender. Add the rice and shrimp, cover, and cook 5 minutes.

4. Remove from the heat and stir in the sausage, salt, and pepper. Cover tightly and let stand 5 minutes or until the liquid is absorbed.

EXCHANGES / CHOICES

2 Starch
1 Nonstarchy Vegetable
2 Protein, lean

Calories	280
Calories from Fat	50
Total Fat	6.0 g
Saturated Fat	1.7 g
Trans Fat	0.1 g
Cholesterol	115 mg
Sodium	370 mg
Potassium	400 mg
Total Carbohydrate	35 g
Dietary Fiber	3 g
Sugars	3 g
Protein	21 g
Phosphorus	305 mg

COOK'S TIP

The sausage is added at the very end of the cooking process for enhanced flavor.

Tilapia Stew with Green Peppers
page 83

Tuna Steaks with Garlic Aioli

SERVES 4 ■ **SERVING SIZE** 1 steak plus 2 tablespoons sauce
PREP TIME 5 minutes ■ **COOK TIME** 6 minutes

1/4 cup reduced-fat mayonnaise

1/4 cup fat-free sour cream

1/2 teaspoon minced garlic

1/4 teaspoon salt (divided use)

1/2 teaspoon black pepper

4 (4-ounce) tuna steaks, rinsed and patted dry

1 Preheat the grill over high heat, or preheat the broiler.

2 Stir the mayonnaise, sour cream, garlic, and 1/4 teaspoon salt together in a small bowl and set aside.

3 Sprinkle 1/4 teaspoon salt and the pepper over the steaks. Coat the grill or broiler rack and pan with nonstick cooking spray. Grill or broil the steaks 3 minutes on each side or until they are done as desired.

4 Serve the sauce alongside the steaks.

EXCHANGES / CHOICES

4 Protein, lean
1/2 Fat

Calories	220
Calories from Fat	90
Total Fat	10.0 g
Saturated Fat	2.0 g
Trans Fat	0.0 g
Cholesterol	50 mg
Sodium	330 mg
Potassium	330 mg
Total Carbohydrate	4 g
Dietary Fiber	0 g
Sugars	2 g
Protein	28 g
Phosphorus	320 mg

COOK'S TIP

Fresh tuna should be grilled very lightly, so that it's still very pink in the center, for peak flavor and texture. Be careful not to overcook it—the tuna dries out and loses flavor very quickly.

Salmon with Lemon-Thyme Slices

SERVES 4 ■ **SERVING SIZE** 1 filet ■ **PREP TIME** 5 minutes ■ **COOK TIME** 10–12 minutes

2 medium lemons

4 (4-ounce) salmon filets, rinsed and patted dry, skinned (if desired)

1/2 teaspoon dried thyme, crushed

1/4 teaspoon salt

1/4 teaspoon black pepper

1 Preheat the oven to 400°F.

2 Line a baking sheet with foil and coat with nonstick cooking spray. Slice one of the lemons into 8 rounds and arrange on the baking sheet.

3 Place the salmon on top of the lemon slices, spray the salmon lightly with nonstick cooking spray, and sprinkle evenly with the thyme, salt, and pepper. Bake the salmon 10–12 minutes or until it flakes with a fork.

4 Cut the other lemon in quarters and squeeze lemon juice evenly over all.

EXCHANGES / CHOICES

3 Protein, lean
1 Fat

Calories	180
Calories from Fat	80
Total Fat	9.0 g
Saturated Fat	1.8 g
Trans Fat	0.0 g
Cholesterol	60 mg
Sodium	220 mg
Potassium	440 mg
Total Carbohydrate	3 g
Dietary Fiber	1 g
Sugars	1 g
Protein	22 g
Phosphorus	295 mg

COOK'S TIP

Using the lemon slices as a "bed" for the salmon to cook on not only prevents the delicate fish from sticking to the foil, but allows the oils from the lemon rind to penetrate into the salmon, giving it great lemony flavor.

VEGETARIAN DISHES

Hurried Hummus Wraps

SERVES 4 ■ **SERVING SIZE** 2 wrap halves ■ **PREP TIME** 5 minutes

4 whole-wheat flour tortillas

1/2 cup prepared hummus

6 cups packed mixed greens or
spring greens

2 ounces crumbled reduced-fat feta or
reduced-fat bleu cheese

1 Warm tortillas according to package directions.

2 Top each with 2 tablespoons hummus, 1 1/2 cups lettuce, and 2 tablespoons cheese, roll tightly and cut in half.

EXCHANGES / CHOICES

1 Vegetable
1 1/2 Starch
2 Fat

Calories	210
Calories from Fat	130
Total Fat	14 g
Saturated Fat	2.7 g
Trans Fat	0 g
Cholesterol	5 mg
Sodium	420 mg
Potassium	385 mg
Total Carbohydrate	28 g
Dietary Fiber	4 g
Sugars	1 g
Protein	8 g
Phosphorus	140 mg

Open-Faced Grilled Pepper-Goat Cheese Sandwiches

SERVES 4 ■ **SERVING SIZE** 2 bread slices, 1/2 cup pepper mixture, and 2 tablespoons crumbled cheese
PREP TIME 5 minutes ■ **COOK TIME** 25 minutes

3 large red bell peppers, halved
   lengthwise

1 1/2 tablespoons balsamic vinegar

8 ounces whole grain loaf bread,
   cut in half lengthwise

2 ounces crumbled goat cheese

1 Heat grill or grill pan over medium-high heat. Flatten pepper halves with palm of hand. Coat both sides with cooking spray and cook 20 minutes or until tender, turning frequently. Place on cutting board and coarsely chop. Combine the peppers with the vinegar and 1/8 teaspoon salt, if desired. Cover to keep warm.

2 Coat both sides of the bread with cooking spray and cook 1 1/2 to 2 minutes on each side or until lightly browned. Cut each bread half crosswise into 4 pieces.

3 Top each bread slice with 1/4 cup pepper mixture and sprinkle cheese evenly over all.

EXCHANGES / CHOICES

1 Nonstarchy Vegetable
2 Starch
1/2 Protein, high fat

Calories	250
Calories from Fat	60
Total Fat	7 g
Saturated Fat	3.3 g
Trans Fat	0 g
Cholesterol	10 mg
Sodium	280 mg
Potassium	410 mg
Total Carbohydrate	33 g
Dietary Fiber	7 g
Sugars	10 g
Protein	12 g
Phosphorus	225 mg

COOK'S TIP
May add 1/3 cup chopped fresh basil to the pepper mixture, if desired.

COOK'S TIP
Don't worry if the peppers split while flattening them.

Toasted Grain and Arugula

SERVES 4 ■ **SERVING SIZE** 1 cup ■ **PREP TIME** 5 minutes ■ **COOK TIME** 20 minutes

4 ounces slivered almonds

1 cup dry bulgur

4 cups arugula

1/2 cup lite balsamic salad dressing

1 Heat a large skillet over medium-high heat. Add the almonds and cook 2 minutes or until beginning to lightly brown, stirring constantly. Set aside on separate plate.

2 Add the bulgur to the skillet and cook (in the dry skillet) 3 minutes or until beginning to lightly brown, stirring constantly. Add 2 cups water, bring to a boil, reduce heat to low, cover, and simmer 12 minutes or until liquid is absorbed.

3 Remove from heat, place in a bowl with the arugula, 1/8 teaspoon salt, and 1/8 teaspoon pepper, if desired. Toss until arugula is slightly wilted.

4 Add the dressing to the skillet. Bring to a boil over medium-high heat and cook 2 minutes or until reduced to 1/3 cup. Immediately pour over the bulgur mixture and toss until well blended.

EXCHANGES / CHOICES
1 Nonstarchy Vegetable
2 Starch
3 Fat

Calories	310
Calories from Fat	60
Total Fat	16 g
Saturated Fat	1.4 g
Trans Fat	0.0 g
Cholesterol	0 mg
Sodium	380 mg
Potassium	420 mg
Total Carbohydrate	39 g
Dietary Fiber	10 g
Sugars	3 g
Protein	11 g
Phosphorus	250 mg

Zucchini on Bleu Cheese Pasta

SERVES 4 ■ **SERVING SIZE** 3/4 cup pasta and 3/4 cup vegetables
PREP TIME 5 minutes ■ **COOK TIME** 15 minutes

6 ounces uncooked whole-grain rotini pasta

2 medium zucchini squash

4 whole green onions, ends trimmed

2 ounces reduced-fat bleu cheese, crumbled

3/8 teaspoon salt, divided use

1/8 teaspoon pepper

1 Cook pasta according to package directions. Drain and reserve 1/4 cup pasta water.

2 Meanwhile, heat a grill pan or skillet over medium-high heat. Cut zucchini in quarters lengthwise. Then cut each quarter in half crosswise (creating 8 pieces total). Coat the zucchini and green onions with cooking spray.

3 Cook zucchini 5 minutes, turning occasionally. Add the green onions and cook another 5 minutes or until zucchini is just tender, turning occasionally.

4 Toss pasta with the bleu cheese, reserved 1/4 cup pasta water, 1/4 teaspoon salt, and 1/8 teaspoon pepper. Top with the zucchini and onions. Top with 1/8 teaspoon salt.

EXCHANGES / CHOICES

2 Nonstarchy Vegetables
1 1/2 Starch
1/2 Protein, medium fat

Calories	210
Calories from Fat	30
Total Fat	3 g
Saturated Fat	1.9 g
Trans Fat	0.0 g
Cholesterol	10 mg
Sodium	420 mg
Potassium	495 mg
Total Carbohydrate	38 g
Dietary Fiber	2 g
Sugars	3 g
Protein	12 g
Phosphorus	215 mg

Pesto Potatoes and Edamame Bake

SERVES 4 ■ **SERVING SIZE** about 1 1/4 cups ■ **PREP TIME** 10 minutes ■ **COOK TIME** 1 hour

1 1/2 pounds red potatoes, cut into 1/4-inch-thick slices

1 cup fresh or frozen, thawed shelled edamame

1/2 cup prepared basil pesto

1/4 cup salted hulled pumpkin seeds

1 Preheat oven to 350°F.

2 Coat a 2-quart baking dish with cooking spray. Arrange half of the potatoes on bottom of baking dish, overlapping slightly. Spoon half of the pesto evenly over all, top with the edamame, sprinkle with 1/4 teaspoon pepper. Repeat with remaining potatoes and pesto.

3 Cover and bake 55 minutes or until tender. Sprinkle with pumpkin seeds and bake, uncovered, 5 minutes.

EXCHANGES / CHOICES

2 Starch
1 Protein, medium-fat
3 1/2 Fat

Calories	370
Calories from Fat	200
Total Fat	22 g
Saturated Fat	3.7 g
Trans Fat	0.0 g
Cholesterol	5 mg
Sodium	380 mg
Potassium	1050 mg
Total Carbohydrate	33 g
Dietary Fiber	2 g
Sugars	3 g
Protein	14 g
Phosphorus	375 mg

COOK'S TIP

Be sure to use red potatoes (or Yukon Gold) for peak texture.

Feta Basil Pasta

SERVES 4 ■ **SERVING SIZE** 1 1/2 cups ■ **PREP TIME** 5 minutes ■ **COOK TIME** 15 minutes

6 ounces whole-grain spaghetti, broken in half

4 ounces crumbled reduced-fat feta cheese

1/2 cup chopped fresh basil

1 cup grape tomatoes, quartered

1 Cook pasta according to package directions, and drain.

2 Place pasta in a shallow bowl or rimmed platter. Top with the remaining ingredients in the order listed and sprinkle with 1/8 teaspoon salt and 1/8 teaspoon pepper, if desired.

EXCHANGES / CHOICES

2 Starch
1 Protein, low-fat

Calories	200
Calories from Fat	20
Total Fat	2.5 g
Saturated Fat	0.7 g
Trans Fat	0.0 g
Cholesterol	5 mg
Sodium	250 mg
Potassium	205 mg
Total Carbohydrate	34 g
Dietary Fiber	1 g
Sugars	1 g
Protein	14 g
Phosphorus	260 mg

Zucchini on Bleu
Cheese Pasta

page 152

Speedy Greek Orzo Salad

SERVES 9 ■ **SERVING SIZE** 1/2 cup ■ **PREP TIME** 4 minutes
COOK TIME 7 minutes ■ **CHILL TIME** 1 hour

8 ounces uncooked whole-wheat orzo pasta

1/2 cup reduced-fat olive oil vinaigrette salad dressing (divided use)

3 tablespoons salt-free Greek seasoning (sold in jars in the spice aisle)

2 ounces crumbled, reduced-fat, sun-dried tomato and basil feta cheese

2 tablespoons chopped fresh parsley (optional)

1 Cook the pasta according to package directions, omitting any salt and fat.

2 Meanwhile, stir 1/4 cup salad dressing and the Greek seasoning together in a medium bowl.

3 Drain the pasta in a colander and run under cold water until cooled. Shake off excess liquid and add it to the salad dressing mixture. Toss well, then add the feta and toss gently. Cover the bowl with plastic wrap and refrigerate at least 1 hour.

4 At serving time, add 1/4 cup salad dressing and toss to coat. Sprinkle with 2 tablespoons chopped fresh parsley, if desired.

EXCHANGES / CHOICES
1 1/2 Starch
1/2 Fat

Calories	130
Calories from Fat	40
Total Fat	4.5 g
Saturated Fat	1.3 g
Trans Fat	0.0 g
Cholesterol	5 mg
Sodium	180 mg
Potassium	85 mg
Total Carbohydrate	20 g
Dietary Fiber	5 g
Sugars	1 g
Protein	4 g
Phosphorus	90 mg

COOK'S TIP
Greek seasoning in jars contains dried oregano, mint, garlic, and other herbs. Don't confuse it with the Greek seasoning blend that contains salt.

Light Parmesan Pasta

SERVES 4 ■ **SERVING SIZE** 1 cup ■ **PREP TIME** 5 minutes ■ **COOK TIME** 8 minutes

8 ounces uncooked whole-wheat no-yolk egg noodles

1/4–1/3 cup fat-free evaporated milk

6 tablespoons grated Parmesan cheese (divided use)

1 tablespoon no-trans-fat margarine (35% vegetable oil)

1/2 teaspoon salt

1/4 teaspoon black pepper

1. Cook the pasta according to package directions, omitting any salt or fat.

2. Drain the pasta well and place it in a medium bowl. Add the remaining ingredients except 1 tablespoon Parmesan cheese. Toss to blend, then sprinkle with 1 tablespoon Parmesan on top.

EXCHANGES / CHOICES

3 Starch
1 Protein, lean

Calories	230
Calories from Fat	35
Total Fat	4.0 g
Saturated Fat	1.5 g
Trans Fat	0.0 g
Cholesterol	5 mg
Sodium	450 mg
Potassium	180 mg
Total Carbohydrate	44 g
Dietary Fiber	6 g
Sugars	2 g
Protein	12 g
Phosphorus	225 mg

COOK'S TIP
Evaporated milk gives a creamier, deeper flavor than other milk varieties—try it whenever you want an especially rich dish.

"Refried" Bean and Rice Casserole

SERVES 4 ■ **SERVING SIZE** 3/4 cup ■ **PREP TIME** 10 minutes ■ **COOK TIME** 15 minutes

2 1/4 cups cooked brown rice (omit added salt or fat)

1 (15.5-ounce) can dark red kidney beans, rinsed and drained

7 tablespoons picante sauce

1/4 cup water

1/2 cup shredded, reduced-fat, sharp cheddar cheese

1 Preheat the oven to 350°F.

2 Coat an 8-inch-square baking pan with nonstick cooking spray. Place the rice in the pan and set aside.

3 Add the beans, picante sauce, and water to a blender and blend until pureed, scraping the sides of the blender frequently.

4 Spread the bean mixture evenly over the rice and sprinkle with cheese. Bake, uncovered, for 15 minutes or until thoroughly heated.

EXCHANGES / CHOICES

3 Starch
1 Protein, lean

Calories	260
Calories from Fat	30
Total Fat	3.5 g
Saturated Fat	1.7 g
Trans Fat	0.0 g
Cholesterol	5 mg
Sodium	430 mg
Potassium	430 mg
Total Carbohydrate	44 g
Dietary Fiber	7 g
Sugars	1 g
Protein	14 g
Phosphorus	275 mg

COOK'S TIP

The refried bean, picante sauce, and water mixture makes a great fat-free bean dip, too! Try topping with reduced-fat, shredded cheddar cheese and serve with warm tortilla chips.

Cheesy Tortilla Rounds

SERVES 4 ■ **SERVING SIZE** 1 tortilla round ■ **PREP TIME** 15 minutes ■ **COOK TIME** 14 minutes

4 (6-inch) soft corn tortillas

1 cup fat-free refried beans

1/2 cup shredded, reduced-fat mozzarella cheese

1 poblano chili pepper, seeded and thinly sliced, or 2 jalapeño chili peppers, seeded and thinly sliced

1 Preheat the broiler.

2 Place a large nonstick skillet over medium-high heat until hot. Coat the skillet with nonstick cooking spray. Place two tortillas in the skillet and cook 1 minute or until they begin to lightly brown on the bottom. Turn them and cook 1 minute, then place on a baking sheet. Repeat with the other two tortillas.

3 Return the skillet to medium-high heat, coat with nonstick cooking spray, and add the peppers. Coat the peppers with nonstick cooking spray and cook 6 minutes or until they are tender and brown, stirring frequently. Remove them from the heat.

4 Spread equal amounts of beans evenly on each tortilla. Broil 4 inches away from the heat source for 1 minute. Sprinkle the cheese and pepper slices evenly over each tortilla and broil another 2 minutes or until the cheese has melted. Serve with lime wedges, if desired.

EXCHANGES / CHOICES

1 1/2 Starch
1 Protein, lean

Calories	150
Calories from Fat	30
Total Fat	3.5 g
Saturated Fat	1.7 g
Trans Fat	0.0 g
Cholesterol	10 mg
Sodium	370 mg
Potassium	320 mg
Total Carbohydrate	23 g
Dietary Fiber	5 g
Sugars	2 g
Protein	9 g
Phosphorus	225 mg

COOK'S TIP

For a spicier dish, use seeded jalapeños rather than the milder poblano peppers.

Open-Faced Grilled Pepper–
Goat Cheese Sandwich
page 150

Country Vegetable and Thyme Quiche

SERVES 4 ■ **SERVING SIZE** about 1 cup ■ **PREP TIME** 5 minutes
COOK TIME 35 minutes ■ **STAND TIME** 10 minutes

1 pound frozen corn and vegetable blend (or your favorite vegetable blend), thawed

1/2 teaspoon dried thyme

1/4 teaspoon salt

1/4 teaspoon black pepper

1 1/2 cups egg substitute

1/2 cup shredded, reduced-fat, sharp cheddar cheese

1 Preheat the oven to 350°F.

2 Coat a 9-inch deep-dish pie pan with nonstick cooking spray. Place the vegetables in the pan and sprinkle them evenly with thyme, salt, and pepper. Pour egg substitute over the vegetables and bake 35 minutes or until just set.

3 Remove the quiche from the oven, sprinkle evenly with the cheese, and let stand 10 minutes to melt the cheese and let the quiche set.

EXCHANGES / CHOICES

1 Starch
2 Protein, lean

Calories	150
Calories from Fat	20
Total Fat	2.5 g
Saturated Fat	1.5 g
Trans Fat	0.0 g
Cholesterol	5 mg
Sodium	430 mg
Potassium	330 mg
Total Carbohydrate	16 g
Dietary Fiber	5 g
Sugars	4 g
Protein	16 g
Phosphorus	140 mg

COOK'S TIP

To thaw frozen vegetables quickly, place them in a colander and run under cold water for 20–30 seconds. Shake off any excess liquid before adding them to the pie pan.

Tomato Topper Over Anything

SERVES 3 ▪ **SERVING SIZE** 1/2 cup ▪ **PREP TIME** 4 minutes
COOK TIME 22 minutes ▪ **STAND TIME** 5 minutes

1 (14.5-ounce) can no-salt-added tomatoes with green pepper and onion

1/2 cup chopped roasted red peppers

2–3 tablespoons chopped fresh basil

2 teaspoons extra virgin olive oil

1. Bring the tomatoes and peppers to boil in a medium saucepan. Reduce the heat and simmer, uncovered, for 15 minutes or until slightly thickened, stirring occasionally.

2. Remove the mixture from the heat, stir in the basil and oil, and let stand 5 minutes to develop flavors.

EXCHANGES / CHOICES
2 Nonstarchy Vegetable
1/2 Fat

Calories	80
Calories from Fat	25
Total Fat	3.0 g
Saturated Fat	0.4 g
Trans Fat	0.0 g
Cholesterol	0 mg
Sodium	90 mg
Potassium	270 mg
Total Carbohydrate	12 g
Dietary Fiber	2 g
Sugars	8 g
Protein	2 g
Phosphorus	25 mg

COOK'S TIP
This recipe doubles easily, and is delicious served over whole-wheat pasta or steamed veggies (top with a little reduced-fat, shredded cheddar cheese to boost the protein).

Broccoli and Toasted Nut Pilaf

SERVES 5 ■ **SERVING SIZE** 1 1/4 cups ■ **PREP TIME** 5 minutes
COOK TIME 28 minutes ■ **STAND TIME** 2–3 minutes

2/3 cup pecan pieces

1 (6-ounce) package long grain and
 wild rice with seasonings

2 cups frozen broccoli florets, thawed

2 cups frozen corn kernels, thawed

1/2 cup water

1/8 teaspoon salt

1/8 teaspoon black pepper

1 Place a medium saucepan over medium heat until hot.
Add the nuts and cook 2–3 minutes or until they begin
to lightly brown and smell fragrant, stirring frequently.
Place them on a plate and set aside.

2 Add the amount of water called for on the rice
package to the saucepan. Bring to a boil, then
add the rice and seasonings. Return to a boil, reduce
the heat, cover tightly, and cook 20 minutes. Add the
broccoli, corn, and water to the rice and stir. Cover
and cook another 5 minutes or until the broccoli is
just tender.

3 Remove the rice from the heat and add the pecans,
salt, and pepper. Let stand 2–3 minutes if any liquid
remains in the pot.

EXCHANGES / CHOICES

2 1/2 Starch
1 Nonstarchy Vegetable
1 1/2 Fat

Calories	280
Calories from Fat	110
Total Fat	12.0 g
Saturated Fat	1.0 g
Trans Fat	0.0 g
Cholesterol	0 mg
Sodium	450 mg
Potassium	390 mg
Total Carbohydrate	39 g
Dietary Fiber	4 g
Sugars	4 g
Protein	7 g
Phosphorus	245 mg

COOK'S TIP

For an even more protein-packed dish, substitute frozen,
shelled edamame (green soybeans) for the broccoli.

Black Bean and Corn Bowl

SERVES 4 ■ **SERVING SIZE** 1 1/4 cups plus 2 tablespoons sour cream
PREP TIME 4 minutes ■ **COOK TIME** 22 minutes

1 (10.5-ounce) can mild tomatoes with green chilis

1 (15-ounce) can black beans, rinsed and drained

2 cups frozen corn kernels

1/4 cup reduced-fat sour cream

1 Place all ingredients except the sour cream in a large saucepan. Bring to a boil over high heat, then reduce the heat, cover, and simmer 20 minutes.

2 Serve in 4 individual bowls topped with 1 tablespoon sour cream.

EXCHANGES / CHOICES

2 Starch
1 Protein, lean

Calories	170
Calories from Fat	20
Total Fat	2.0 g
Saturated Fat	1.2 g
Trans Fat	0.0 g
Cholesterol	5 mg
Sodium	310 mg
Potassium	520 mg
Total Carbohydrate	31 g
Dietary Fiber	7 g
Sugars	6 g
Protein	9 g
Phosphorus	160 mg

COOK'S TIP

Don't confuse the 10.5-ounce can of tomatoes with green chilis with the 14.5-ounce can of tomatoes with Mexican seasonings. The smaller can has a bit more spice and a fresher flavor.

Skillet-Grilled Meatless Burgers with Spicy Sour Cream

SERVES 4 ■ **SERVING SIZE** 1 burger ■ **PREP TIME** 8 minutes ■ **COOK TIME** 15 minutes

4 soy protein burgers (preferably the grilled variety)

1 1/2 cups thinly sliced onions

1/8 teaspoon salt (divided use)

1/4 cup fat-free sour cream

4–6 drops chipotle-flavored hot sauce

1. Place a large nonstick skillet over medium heat until hot. Coat the skillet with nonstick cooking spray, add the patties, and cook 4 minutes on each side. Set the patties aside on a separate plate and cover with foil to keep warm.

2. Coat the skillet with nonstick cooking spray and increase the heat to medium high. Add the onions and 1/16 teaspoon salt. Lightly coat the onions with nonstick cooking spray and cook 5 minutes or until they are richly browned, stirring frequently.

3. Meanwhile, stir the sour cream, hot sauce, and 1/16 teaspoon salt together in a small bowl.

4. When the onions are browned, push them to one side of the skillet and add the patties. Spoon the onions on top of the patties and cook 1–2 minutes longer to heat thoroughly. Top each patty with 1 tablespoon sour cream.

EXCHANGES / CHOICES

1/2 Carbohydrate
1 Nonstarchy Vegetable
2 Protein, lean

Calories	120
Calories from Fat	20
Total Fat	2.0 g
Saturated Fat	0.6 g
Trans Fat	0.0 g
Cholesterol	5 mg
Sodium	440 mg
Potassium	510 mg
Total Carbohydrate	12 g
Dietary Fiber	7 g
Sugars	2 g
Protein	16 g
Phosphorus	270 mg

COOK'S TIP

If you can't find chipotle-flavored hot sauce, you can use 1/2 to 3/4 teaspoon of the adobo sauce that is packed with chipotle chili peppers.

POTATOES, PASTA, AND WHOLE GRAINS

Paprika Roasted Potatoes

SERVES 4 ■ **SERVING SIZE** 1/2 cup ■ **PREP TIME** 5 minutes
COOK TIME 20 minutes ■ **STAND TIME** 10 minutes

12 ounces new potatoes, scrubbed and quartered

1 teaspoon extra virgin olive oil

1/4 teaspoon paprika

1/8 plus 1/4 teaspoon salt (divided use)

1 Preheat the oven to 350°F.

2 Arrange the potatoes on a baking pan lined with foil. Drizzle the oil over the potatoes and toss to coat completely. Sprinkle the potatoes with paprika and 1/8 teaspoon salt and bake for 20 minutes, shaking the pan after 10 minutes to stir.

3 Remove the pan from the oven and sprinkle the potatoes with 1/4 teaspoon salt. Wrap the pan tightly with foil and let stand 10 minutes.

EXCHANGES / CHOICES

1 Starch

Calories	70
Calories from Fat	10
Total Fat	1.0 g
Saturated Fat	0.2 g
Trans Fat	0.0 g
Cholesterol	0 mg
Sodium	220 mg
Potassium	330 mg
Total Carbohydrate	14 g
Dietary Fiber	2 g
Sugars	1 g
Protein	2 g
Phosphorus	45 mg

COOK'S TIP

Wrapping the potatoes with the foil at the end allows the flavors to develop and keeps the potatoes moist.

Parmesan Potato Bake

SERVES 6 ■ **SERVING SIZE** 2/3 cup ■ **PREP TIME** 12 minutes
COOK TIME 1 hour ■ **STAND TIME** 10 minutes

1 1/2 pounds red potatoes, scrubbed and very thinly sliced

1/2 cup finely chopped onion

3 tablespoons no-trans-fat margarine (35% vegetable oil; divided use)

1/8 teaspoon black pepper (divided use)

3 tablespoons grated Parmesan cheese (divided use)

1/4 teaspoon salt (divided use)

1 Preheat the oven to 375°F.

2 Coat a 9-inch deep-dish pie pan with nonstick cooking spray. Put half the potatoes in the pan, then all of the onions, then half of the remaining ingredients. Place the remaining potatoes on top, add the remaining margarine, and sprinkle with the remaining pepper. Cover with foil and bake 45 minutes.

3 Uncover the potatoes and sprinkle with the remaining Parmesan cheese and salt. Bake uncovered for 15 minutes or until the potatoes are tender when pierced with a fork. Let stand 10 minutes to develop flavors.

EXCHANGES / CHOICES

1 1/2 Starch
1/2 Fat

Calories	120
Calories from Fat	25
Total Fat	3.0 g
Saturated Fat	0.9 g
Trans Fat	0.0 g
Cholesterol	0 mg
Sodium	190 mg
Potassium	530 mg
Total Carbohydrate	20 g
Dietary Fiber	2 g
Sugars	2 g
Protein	3 g
Phosphorus	90 mg

COOK'S TIP

To slice potatoes easily and quickly, use a food processor with a slicing attachment.

Chunky Potato and Onion Mash

SERVES 4 ■ **SERVING SIZE** 1/2 cup ■ **PREP TIME** 10 minutes ■ **COOK TIME** 14 minutes

12 ounces red potatoes, scrubbed
  and diced

1/3–1/2 cup fat-free evaporated milk

1/4 cup minced green onion
  (white part only)

2 tablespoons no-trans-fat margarine
  (35% vegetable oil)

1/4 teaspoon salt

1/8 teaspoon black pepper

1 Bring water to boil in a large saucepan. Add the potatoes and return to a boil. Reduce the heat, cover tightly, and simmer 12 minutes or until very tender.

2 Drain the potatoes in a colander and return them to the saucepan. Gradually add the milk, stirring with a whisk until blended. Stir in the remaining ingredients.

EXCHANGES / CHOICES

1 Starch
1/2 Fat

Calories	110
Calories from Fat	20
Total Fat	2.5 g
Saturated Fat	0.6 g
Trans Fat	0.0 g
Cholesterol	0 mg
Sodium	220 mg
Potassium	400 mg
Total Carbohydrate	19 g
Dietary Fiber	2 g
Sugars	3 g
Protein	3 g
Phosphorus	80 mg

COOK'S TIP

If you don't have red potatoes, just use unpeeled baking potatoes instead. Leaving the skins on means greater flavor, more fiber, and less work!

Lemony Beans and Potatoes

SERVES 4 ■ **SERVING SIZE** rounded 3/4 cup ■ **PREP TIME** 10 minutes ■ **COOK TIME** 8 minutes

8 ounces green beans, trimmed and broken into 2-inch pieces

6 ounces new potatoes, scrubbed and quartered

1 teaspoon lemon zest

1 1/2 tablespoons no-trans-fat margarine (35% vegetable oil)

1/4 teaspoon salt

1 Steam the beans and potatoes 7 minutes or until the potatoes are just tender.

2 Place the vegetables in a decorative bowl, add the remaining ingredients, and toss gently. Serve immediately for peak flavor.

EXCHANGES / CHOICES

1/2 Starch
1 Nonstarchy Vegetable

Calories	70
Calories from Fat	20
Total Fat	2.0 g
Saturated Fat	0.4 g
Trans Fat	0.0 g
Cholesterol	0 mg
Sodium	180 mg
Potassium	230 mg
Total Carbohydrate	12 g
Dietary Fiber	2 g
Sugars	1 g
Protein	2 g
Phosphorus	35 mg

COOK'S TIP

This dish also looks great prepared with whole beans— delicious with fresh summer beans.

Country Stuffed
Summer Squash
page 178

Roasted Sweet Potatoes
with Cinnamon

SERVES 4 ■ **SERVING SIZE** 1/2 cup ■ **PREP TIME** 10 minutes
COOK TIME 15 minutes ■ **STAND TIME** 15 minutes

1 pound sweet potatoes, peeled and
cut into 3/4-inch pieces

1 tablespoon canola oil

1 tablespoon sugar

1/2 teaspoon ground cinnamon

1/8 teaspoon salt

1 Preheat the oven to 425°F.

2 Arrange the potatoes on a baking pan lined with a
foil. Drizzle the oil over the potatoes and toss to coat
completely. Bake 10 minutes, then shake pan to stir.
Bake another 5 minutes or until the potatoes are
tender when pierced with a fork.

3 Meanwhile, stir the remaining ingredients together in
a small bowl.

4 Remove the pan from the oven and sprinkle the
potatoes with the cinnamon mixture. Lift up the ends
of the foil and fold them over the potatoes, sealing the
ends tightly but not pressing down on the potatoes. Let
the potatoes stand 15 minutes to develop flavors and
release moisture.

EXCHANGES / CHOICES
1 Starch
1/2 Fat

Calories	110
Calories from Fat	30
Total Fat	3.5 g
Saturated Fat	0.3 g
Trans Fat	0.0 g
Cholesterol	0 mg
Sodium	95 mg
Potassium	340 mg
Total Carbohydrate	18 g
Dietary Fiber	2 g
Sugars	8 g
Protein	1 g
Phosphorus	40 mg

COOK'S TIP
The tiny bit of salt really helps to blend the flavors. This is
true in many different dishes.

Speed-Dial Sweet Potatoes

SERVES 4 ■ **SERVING SIZE** 1/2 potato plus 1 tablespoon honey mixture
PREP TIME 4 minutes ■ **COOK TIME** 7 minutes

2 (8-ounce) sweet potatoes, scrubbed and pierced several times with a fork

3 tablespoons no-trans-fat margarine (35% vegetable oil)

2 teaspoons honey

1/4 teaspoon vanilla

1/16 teaspoon salt

1 Microwave the potatoes on HIGH for 7 minutes or until they are tender when pierced with a fork.

2 Meanwhile, stir the remaining ingredients together in a small bowl.

3 Split the potatoes in half lengthwise, fluff with a fork, and drizzle 1 tablespoon of the margarine mixture on each half.

EXCHANGES / CHOICES

1 1/2 Starch
1/2 Fat

Calories	130
Calories from Fat	35
Total Fat	4.0 g
Saturated Fat	0.8 g
Trans Fat	0.0 g
Cholesterol	0 mg
Sodium	135 mg
Potassium	440 mg
Total Carbohydrate	22 g
Dietary Fiber	3 g
Sugars	9 g
Protein	2 g
Phosphorus	50 mg

COOK'S TIP

The margarine mixture melts right into the sweet potatoes and looks inviting, with a rich, slightly sweet flavor.

Brown Rice with Pine Nuts

SERVES 4 ■ **SERVING SIZE** 1/2 cup ■ **PREP TIME** 6 minutes ■ **COOK TIME** 16 minutes

3 tablespoons pine nuts

1 cup finely chopped onion

3/4 cup water

1/2 cup instant brown rice

1/4 teaspoon salt

1. Place a medium nonstick skillet over medium-high heat until hot. Add the pine nuts and cook 1–2 minutes or until they begin to lightly brown, stirring constantly. Set them aside on a separate plate.

2. Coat the skillet with nonstick cooking spray and add the onions. Cook for 3–4 minutes or until the onions begin to richly brown, stirring frequently. Set them aside with the pine nuts.

3. Add the water, rice, and salt to the skillet. Bring to a boil over high heat, reduce the heat, cover tightly, and cook 10 minutes or until the water is absorbed.

4. Remove the skillet from the heat and stir in the onions and pine nuts.

EXCHANGES / CHOICES

1 Starch
1 Nonstarchy Vegetable
1 Fat

Calories	150
Calories from Fat	45
Total Fat	5.0 g
Saturated Fat	0.4 g
Trans Fat	0.0 g
Cholesterol	0 mg
Sodium	160 mg
Potassium	160 mg
Total Carbohydrate	23 g
Dietary Fiber	2 g
Sugars	2 g
Protein	3 g
Phosphorus	130 mg

COOK'S TIP

Toasting the pine nuts adds just the right degree of nutty flavor to the rice. Be sure to use a dry skillet—no oil needed.

Rosemary Rice with Fresh Spinach Greens

SERVES 4 ■ **SERVING SIZE** 1/2 cup ■ **PREP TIME** 4 minutes ■ **COOK TIME** 11 minutes

1 1/2 cups water

3/4 cup instant brown rice

1/8–1/4 teaspoon dried rosemary

1 cup packed spinach leaves, coarsely chopped

1 tablespoon no-trans-fat margarine (35% vegetable oil)

1/4 teaspoon salt

1. Bring the water and rice to a boil in a medium saucepan. Add the rice and rosemary, reduce the heat, cover tightly, and simmer 10 minutes.

2. Remove the saucepan from the heat and stir in remaining ingredients. Toss gently, yet thoroughly, until the spinach has wilted.

EXCHANGES / CHOICES

2 Starch

Calories	140
Calories from Fat	20
Total Fat	2.5 g
Saturated Fat	0.4 g
Trans Fat	0.0 g
Cholesterol	0 mg
Sodium	190 mg
Potassium	125 mg
Total Carbohydrate	27 g
Dietary Fiber	2 g
Sugars	0 g
Protein	3 g
Phosphorus	125 mg

COOK'S TIP

For variation, use spring lettuce mix instead of the spinach. It adds a bit of sophistication as well as great color, texture, and flavor.

Taco-Spiced Rice

SERVES 4 ■ **SERVING SIZE** 1/2 cup ■ **PREP TIME** 6 minutes ■ **COOK TIME** 11 minutes

1 1/4 cups water (divided use)

1/2 cup instant brown rice

1 medium red bell pepper, chopped

1 medium onion, chopped

1 tablespoon taco seasoning
  (available in packets)

1 tablespoon no-trans-fat margarine
  (35% vegetable oil), optional

1 Bring 1 cup water and the rice to boil in a small saucepan, then reduce the heat, cover tightly, and simmer 10 minutes.

2 Meanwhile, place a large nonstick skillet over medium-high heat until hot. Coat the skillet with nonstick cooking spray and add the peppers and onions. Coat the vegetables with nonstick cooking spray and cook 5 minutes or until the vegetables are tender-crisp.

3 In a small bowl, dissolve the taco seasoning in 1/4 cup water. Stir into the rice, add the margarine, if desired, and stir until well blended.

EXCHANGES / CHOICES

1 1/2 Starch
1 Nonstarchy Vegetable

Calories	130
Calories from Fat	20
Total Fat	2.0 g
Saturated Fat	0.4 g
Trans Fat	0.0 g
Cholesterol	0 mg
Sodium	200 mg
Potassium	200 mg
Total Carbohydrate	25 g
Dietary Fiber	3 g
Sugars	4 g
Protein	3 g
Phosphorus	110 mg

COOK'S TIP

You'll find the taco seasoning packets next to the taco shells and salsas in the supermarket. Use just a little to give your dishes Southwestern flavor.

Pasta'd Mushrooms

SERVES 4 ■ **SERVING SIZE** 1/2 cup ■ **PREP TIME** 5 minutes ■ **COOK TIME** 10 minutes

2 ounces dry, uncooked, whole-wheat spaghetti noodles, broken into thirds

3/4 cup finely chopped onion

8 ounces sliced mushrooms

1/4 teaspoon salt, divided use

1/8 teaspoon black pepper

2 tablespoons no-trans-fat margarine (35% vegetable oil)

1 Cook the pasta according to package directions, omitting any salt or fat.

2 Meanwhile, place a large nonstick skillet over medium-high heat until hot. Coat the skillet with nonstick cooking spray, add the onions, and cook 3 minutes or until the onions begin to brown, stirring frequently.

3 Add the mushrooms, 1/8 teaspoon salt, and the pepper. Coat the mushroom mixture with nonstick cooking spray and cook 5 minutes longer, stirring frequently. Use two utensils to stir as you would when stir-frying.

4 Remove the skillet from the heat, stir in the margarine, and cover to keep warm.

5 Drain the pasta, reserving a little water, and stir the pasta and 1/8 teaspoon salt into the mushroom mixture. If needed, add a little pasta water to moisten.

EXCHANGES / CHOICES
1/2 Starch
1 Nonstarchy Vegetable
1/2 Fat

Calories	100
Calories from Fat	25
Total Fat	3.0 g
Saturated Fat	0.6 g
Trans Fat	0.0 g
Cholesterol	0 mg
Sodium	190 mg
Potassium	270 mg
Total Carbohydrate	16 g
Dietary Fiber	3 g
Sugars	3 g
Protein	4 g
Phosphorus	95 mg

COOK'S TIP
Using whole-wheat pasta is a great way to add fiber and nutrients to your pasta dishes.

Country Stuffed Summer Squash

SERVES 4 ■ **SERVING SIZE** 1 squash half ■ **PREP TIME** 15 minutes ■ **COOK TIME** 35 minutes

2 large summer squash, halved lengthwise (12 ounces total; use any variety, such as yellow, scallop, or zucchini)

1 cup chopped red or green bell pepper

1/2 cup water

2 tablespoons no-trans-fat margarine (35% vegetable oil)

1 cup dry cornbread stuffing mix

1 Preheat the oven to 350°F.

2 Scoop out and coarsely chop the squash pulp.

3 Place a medium nonstick skillet over medium-high heat until hot. Coat the skillet with nonstick cooking spray and add the squash pulp and bell pepper. Cook 4 minutes or until the pepper is tender-crisp, stirring frequently.

4 Remove the skillet from the heat and stir in the water and margarine. Add the stuffing mix and stir gently with a fork. Spoon 1/2 cup stuffing into each squash half. Press down gently so the stuffing will adhere.

5 Recoat the skillet with nonstick cooking spray, arrange the stuffed squash in the skillet, cover tightly, and bake 30 minutes or until the squash is tender when pierced with a fork.

EXCHANGES / CHOICES

1/2 Starch
1 Nonstarchy Vegetable
1/2 Fat

Calories	100
Calories from Fat	30
Total Fat	3.5 g
Saturated Fat	0.6 g
Trans Fat	0.0 g
Cholesterol	0 mg
Sodium	210 mg
Potassium	320 mg
Total Carbohydrate	16 g
Dietary Fiber	2 g
Sugars	4 g
Protein	3 g
Phosphorus	60 mg

COOK'S TIP

Nonstick skillets will work fine at 350°F, even with plastic handles. You may cover the handle with foil, if you like. Or use a 12 × 8-inch glass baking dish.

Roasted Corn and Peppers with Cumin

SERVES 4 ■ **SERVING SIZE** 1/2 cup ■ **PREP TIME** 3 minutes ■ **COOK TIME** 11 minutes

1 medium red bell pepper, chopped

10 ounces frozen corn kernels

1 tablespoon no-trans-fat margarine (35% vegetable oil)

1/2–3/4 teaspoon ground cumin

1/4 teaspoon salt

1/8 teaspoon black pepper

1 Place a large nonstick skillet over medium-high heat until hot. Coat the skillet with nonstick cooking spray and add the bell peppers. Coat the peppers with nonstick cooking spray and cook 7 minutes or until they begin to richly brown, stirring frequently.

2 Add the corn and cook 3 minutes or until the corn just begins to turn light golden in places, stirring occasionally.

3 Remove the skillet from the heat and stir in the remaining ingredients.

EXCHANGES / CHOICES
1 Starch

Calories	80
Calories from Fat	20
Total Fat	2.0 g
Saturated Fat	0.4 g
Trans Fat	0.0 g
Cholesterol	0 mg
Sodium	170 mg
Potassium	250 mg
Total Carbohydrate	16 g
Dietary Fiber	3 g
Sugars	4 g
Protein	2 g
Phosphorus	65 mg

COOK'S TIP
You can serve this great side dish next to, or on top of, grilled meats and fish.

VEGETABLES AND FRUIT SIDES

Grilled Soy Pepper Petites

SERVES 4 ■ **SERVING SIZE** 1 cup ■ **PREP TIME** 5 minutes ■ **COOK TIME** 12 minutes

1 pound petite peppers

3 tablespoons apricot or raspberry
fruit spread

1 1/2 tablespoons light soy sauce

1/8 to 1/4 teaspoon dried pepper flakes

1. Heat a grill or grill pan over medium-high heat. Coat peppers with cooking spray and cook 12 minutes or until tender and beginning to char, turning frequently.

2. Meanwhile, heat fruit spread in microwave for 15 seconds to melt slightly; whisk in soy sauce and pepper flakes.

3. Place peppers in a shallow bowl or rimmed platter and toss with mixture. Serve warm or room temperature.

EXCHANGES / CHOICES

2 Nonstarchy Vegetable

Calories	55
Calories from Fat	0
Total Fat	0 g
Saturated Fat	0 g
Trans Fat	0.0 g
Cholesterol	0 mg
Sodium	200 mg
Potassium	295 mg
Total Carbohydrate	12 g
Dietary Fiber	2 g
Sugars	9 g
Protein	2 g
Phosphorus	40 mg

COOK'S TIP

If the peppers are allowed to "sit" in the fruit spread mixture 15 minutes, the sauce begins to thicken slightly, creating a light glaze or sauce.

COOK'S TIP

This makes a great appetizer as well as an interesting, inviting side dish!

Fresh Lemon Roasted Brussels Sprouts

SERVES 4 ■ **SERVING SIZE** 3/4 cup ■ **PREP TIME** 5 minutes ■ **COOK TIME** 20 minutes

1 pound fresh Brussels sprouts, ends trimmed and halved

2 tablespoons extra-virgin olive oil, divided

Juice and zest of 1 medium lemon

2 teaspoons Worcestershire sauce

1/4 teaspoon pepper

1 Preheat oven 425°F.

2 Toss Brussels sprouts with 1 tablespoon oil, place in a single layer on a foil-lined baking sheet. Roast 10 minutes, stir, and cook 10 minutes or until just tender and beginning to brown.

3 Remove, toss with remaining ingredients and 1/4 teaspoon salt, if desired.

EXCHANGES / CHOICES
2 1/2 Nonstarchy Vegetable
1 1/2 Fat

Calories	115
Calories from Fat	60
Total Fat	7.0 g
Saturated Fat	1.0 g
Trans Fat	0.0 g
Cholesterol	0 mg
Sodium	55 mg
Potassium	490 mg
Total Carbohydrate	13 g
Dietary Fiber	5 g
Sugars	3 g
Protein	4 g
Phosphorus	85 mg

Roasted Beans and Green Onions

SERVES 4 ■ **SERVING SIZE** 1/2 cup ■ **PREP TIME** 8 minutes ■ **COOK TIME** 11 minutes

8 ounces green string beans, trimmed

4 whole green onions, trimmed and cut in fourths (about 3-inch pieces)

1 1/2 teaspoons extra virgin olive oil

1/4 teaspoon salt

1 Preheat the oven to 425°F.

2 Line a baking sheet with foil and coat the foil with nonstick cooking spray.

3 Toss the beans, onions, and oil together in a medium bowl. Arrange them in a thin layer on the baking sheet.

4 Bake for 8 minutes and stir gently, using two utensils as you would for a stir-fry. Bake another 3–4 minutes or until the beans begin to brown on the edges and are tender-crisp.

5 Remove the pan from the oven and sprinkle the beans with salt.

EXCHANGES / CHOICES
1 Nonstarchy Vegetable

Calories	35
Calories from Fat	20
Total Fat	2.0 g
Saturated Fat	0.3 g
Trans Fat	0.0 g
Cholesterol	0 mg
Sodium	150 mg
Potassium	110 mg
Total Carbohydrate	5 g
Dietary Fiber	2 g
Sugars	1 g
Protein	1 g
Phosphorus	20 mg

COOK'S TIP
This side is a great accompaniment to grilled meats and fish—perfect for patio entertaining.

Broccoli Piquant

SERVES 4 ■ **SERVING SIZE** 3/4 cup ■ **PREP TIME** 5 minutes ■ **COOK TIME** 7 minutes

10 ounces fresh broccoli florets

1 tablespoon no-trans-fat margarine
   (35% vegetable oil)

1 teaspoon Worcestershire sauce

1 teaspoon lemon juice

1/4 teaspoon salt

1 Steam the broccoli for 6 minutes or until the broccoli is tender-crisp.

2 Meanwhile, microwave the remaining ingredients in a small glass bowl on HIGH for 15 seconds. Stir until smooth.

3 Place the broccoli on a serving platter and drizzle the sauce evenly over all.

EXCHANGES / CHOICES
1 Nonstarchy Vegetable

Calories	35
Calories from Fat	15
Total Fat	1.5 g
Saturated Fat	0.3 g
Trans Fat	0.0 g
Cholesterol	0 mg
Sodium	200 mg
Potassium	240 mg
Total Carbohydrate	4 g
Dietary Fiber	2 g
Sugars	2 g
Protein	2 g
Phosphorus	50 mg

COOK'S TIP
The concentrated flavors in the topping go a long way, so a little is all you need.

Buttery Dijon Asparagus

SERVES 4 ■ **SERVING SIZE** 5 asparagus spears ■ **PREP TIME** 5 minutes ■ **COOK TIME** 3 minutes

1 tablespoon no-trans-fat margarine (35% vegetable oil)

1 tablespoon Dijon mustard

1 tablespoon finely chopped fresh parsley

1/8 teaspoon salt

1 cup water

20 asparagus spears, trimmed (about 1 pound)

1. Using a fork, stir the margarine, mustard, parsley, and salt together in a small bowl until well blended.

2. Place the water and asparagus in a large skillet and bring to a boil over high heat. Cover tightly and boil 2–3 minutes or until the asparagus is tender-crisp.

3. Drain the asparagus well and place it on a serving platter. Using the back of a spoon, spread the margarine mixture evenly on the asparagus.

EXCHANGES / CHOICES
1 Nonstarchy Vegetable

Calories	40
Calories from Fat	15
Total Fat	1.5 g
Saturated Fat	0.3 g
Trans Fat	0.0 g
Cholesterol	0 mg
Sodium	190 mg
Potassium	240 mg
Total Carbohydrate	5 g
Dietary Fiber	3 g
Sugars	2 g
Protein	3 g
Phosphorus	65 mg

COOK'S TIP
Try this recipe with finely chopped fresh dill instead of parsley.

Squash Melt

SERVES 4 ■ SERVING SIZE 1/2 cup ■ PREP TIME 5 minutes
COOK TIME 8 minutes ■ STAND TIME 2 minutes

2 medium yellow squash (about
   12 ounces total), cut in 1/8-inch
   rounds

1 medium green bell pepper, chopped
   or 1 cup thinly sliced yellow onion

1/4–1/2 teaspoon dried oregano

1/4 teaspoon salt

1/4 cup shredded, reduced-fat, sharp
   cheddar cheese

1. Place a medium nonstick skillet over medium-high heat until hot. Coat the skillet with nonstick cooking spray and add all the ingredients except the cheese.

2. Coat the vegetables with nonstick cooking spray and cook 6–7 minutes or until the vegetables are tender, stirring constantly. Use two utensils to stir as you would when stir-frying.

3. Remove the skillet from the heat and sprinkle the vegetables evenly with the cheese. Cover and let stand 2 minutes to melt the cheese.

EXCHANGES / CHOICES

1 Nonstarchy Vegetable
1/2 Fat

Calories	40
Calories from Fat	15
Total Fat	1.5 g
Saturated Fat	0.8 g
Trans Fat	0.0 g
Cholesterol	5 mg
Sodium	190 mg
Potassium	300 mg
Total Carbohydrate	5 g
Dietary Fiber	2 g
Sugars	3 g
Protein	3 g
Phosphorus	75 mg

COOK'S TIP

You need to coat this quantity of vegetables with nonstick cooking spray to prevent them from burning.

Mashed Cauliflower with Sour Cream

SERVES 4 ■ **SERVING SIZE** 1/2 cup ■ **PREP TIME** 10 minutes ■ **COOK TIME** 10 minutes

1 cup water

1 pound fresh or frozen cauliflower florets

1/4 cup fat-free sour cream

2 tablespoons no-trans-fat margarine (35% vegetable oil)

1/4 teaspoon salt

1/4 teaspoon black pepper

1 Bring the water to boil in a large saucepan and add the cauliflower. Return to a boil, reduce the heat, cover tightly, and simmer 8 minutes or until tender.

2 Drain the cauliflower well and place it in a blender with the remaining ingredients. Hold the lid down tightly and blend until smooth. You may need to turn off the blender and scrape the mixture off the sides once or twice.

EXCHANGES / CHOICES

1 Nonstarchy Vegetable
1/2 Fat

Calories	60
Calories from Fat	25
Total Fat	3.0 g
Saturated Fat	0.8 g
Trans Fat	0.0 g
Cholesterol	0 mg
Sodium	240 mg
Potassium	360 mg
Total Carbohydrate	8 g
Dietary Fiber	2 g
Sugars	3 g
Protein	3 g
Phosphorus	65 mg

COOK'S TIP
Be sure to hold the blender lid down tightly—the heat of the vegetables may cause it to pop off.

Honey-Buttered Acorn Squash

SERVES 4 ■ **SERVING SIZE** 1 squash quarter plus 1 heaping tablespoon honey mixture
PREP TIME 8 minutes ■ **COOK TIME** 7 minutes

1 1/2-pound acorn squash, quartered and seeded

1/3 cup water

3 tablespoons trans-fat-free margarine (35% vegetable oil)

1 1/2 tablespoons honey

1/4 teaspoon ground nutmeg

1/8 teaspoon salt

1. Pierce the outer skin of the squash in several areas with a fork or the tip of a sharp knife.

2. Place the water in a 9-inch glass pie pan and add the squash, cut side up. Cover with plastic wrap and microwave on HIGH for 7 minutes or until the squash is tender when pierced with a fork.

3. Meanwhile, using a fork, stir the remaining ingredients together in a small bowl until well blended.

4. Place the squash on a serving platter and spoon a heaping tablespoon of the honey mixture on the center of each squash quarter.

EXCHANGES / CHOICES

1 Starch
1/2 Fat

Calories	90
Calories from Fat	35
Total Fat	4.0 g
Saturated Fat	0.9 g
Trans Fat	0.0 g
Cholesterol	0 mg
Sodium	140 mg
Potassium	340 mg
Total Carbohydrate	13 g
Dietary Fiber	3 g
Sugars	6 g
Protein	1 g
Phosphorus	35 mg

COOK'S TIP

The heat of the squash will gradually melt the honey mixture.

Skillet-Roasted Veggies

SERVES 4 ■ **SERVING SIZE** 1/2 cup ■ **PREP TIME** 7 minutes
COOK TIME 6 minutes ■ **STAND TIME** 2 minutes

5 ounces asparagus spears, trimmed and cut into 2-inch pieces (1 cup total), patted dry

3 ounces sliced portobello mushrooms (1/2 of a 6-ounce package)

1/2 medium red bell pepper, cut in thin strips

1/4 teaspoon salt

1/8 teaspoon black pepper

1. Place a large nonstick skillet over medium-high heat until hot. Coat the skillet with nonstick cooking spray and add the asparagus, mushrooms, and bell pepper. Coat the vegetables with nonstick cooking spray and sprinkle evenly with the salt and black pepper.

2. Cook 5–6 minutes, or until the vegetables begin to richly brown on the edges. Use two utensils to stir as you would when stir-frying.

3. Remove from the heat, cover tightly, and let stand 2 minutes to develop flavors.

EXCHANGES / CHOICES
1 Nonstarchy Vegetable

Calories	15
Calories from Fat	5
Total Fat	0.5 g
Saturated Fat	0.1 g
Trans Fat	0.0 g
Cholesterol	0 mg
Sodium	150 mg
Potassium	170 mg
Total Carbohydrate	3 g
Dietary Fiber	1 g
Sugars	1 g
Protein	1 g
Phosphorus	40 mg

COOK'S TIP
Coating the vegetables with nonstick cooking spray helps them to brown without a lot of added fat.

Creole-Simmered Vegetables

SERVES 4 ■ **SERVING SIZE** 1/2 cup ■ **PREP TIME** 4 minutes ■ **COOK TIME** 24 minutes

1 (14.5-ounce) can stewed tomatoes with Cajun seasonings

2 cups frozen pepper and onion stir-fry

3/4 cup thinly sliced celery

1 tablespoon no-trans-fat margarine (35% vegetable oil)

1   Place all the ingredients except the margarine in a medium saucepan and bring to a boil over high heat. Reduce the heat, cover tightly, and simmer 20 minutes or until the onions are very tender.

2   Increase the heat to high and cook 2 minutes, uncovered, to thicken the vegetables slightly. Remove from the heat and stir in the margarine.

EXCHANGES / CHOICES
2 Nonstarchy Vegetable

Calories	60
Calories from Fat	15
Total Fat	1.5 g
Saturated Fat	0.3 g
Trans Fat	0.0 g
Cholesterol	0 mg
Sodium	210 mg
Potassium	310 mg
Total Carbohydrate	10 g
Dietary Fiber	2 g
Sugars	6 g
Protein	2 g
Phosphorus	35 mg

COOK'S TIP
For a nice change, serve this as a bedding for grilled chicken or fish.

Saucy Eggplant and Capers

SERVES 4 ■ **SERVING SIZE** 1/2 cup ■ **PREP TIME** 8 minutes
COOK TIME 21 minutes ■ **STAND TIME** 3 minutes

10 ounces eggplant, diced
(about 2 1/2 cups)

1 (14.5-ounce) can stewed tomatoes
with Italian seasonings

2 tablespoons chopped fresh basil

2 teaspoons capers, drained

2 teaspoons extra virgin olive oil
(optional)

1 Bring the eggplant and tomatoes to boil in a large saucepan over high heat. Reduce the heat, cover tightly, and simmer 20 minutes or until the eggplant is very tender.

2 Remove the saucepan from the heat, stir in the basil, capers, and 2 teaspoons extra virgin olive oil (if desired), and let stand 3 minutes to develop flavors.

EXCHANGES / CHOICES
2 Nonstarchy Vegetable

Calories	50
Calories from Fat	5
Total Fat	0.5 g
Saturated Fat	0.1 g
Trans Fat	0.0 g
Cholesterol	0 mg
Sodium	250 mg
Potassium	380 mg
Total Carbohydrate	12 g
Dietary Fiber	3 g
Sugars	7 g
Protein	2 g
Phosphorus	40 mg

COOK'S TIP
Adding the basil and capers at the very end gives these vegetables extra punch, with the flavors "on top" more pronounced.

Buttery Tarragon Sugar Snaps

SERVES 4 ■ **SERVING SIZE** 1/2 cup ■ **PREP TIME** 4 minutes ■ **COOK TIME** 8 minutes

8 ounces sugar snap peas, trimmed

1 1/2 tablespoons no-trans-fat margarine (35% vegetable oil)

1 tablespoon chopped fresh parsley

1/2 teaspoon dried tarragon

1/4 teaspoon salt

1 Steam the sugar snaps for 6 minutes or until they are tender-crisp.

2 Place them in a serving bowl, add the remaining ingredients, and toss gently.

EXCHANGES / CHOICES

1 Nonstarchy Vegetable
1/2 Fat

Calories	45
Calories from Fat	20
Total Fat	2.0 g
Saturated Fat	0.4 g
Trans Fat	0.0 g
Cholesterol	0 mg
Sodium	180 mg
Potassium	80 mg
Total Carbohydrate	5 g
Dietary Fiber	1 g
Sugars	2 g
Protein	1 g
Phosphorus	30 mg

COOK'S TIP

Fresh sugar snap peas are available in the spring and fall, but you can find them year-round in the frozen vegetable aisle. They're a delicious cross of sweet peas and snow peas.

Green Pea and Red Pepper Toss

SERVES 4 ■ **SERVING SIZE** 1/2 cup ■ **PREP TIME** 4 minutes ■ **COOK TIME** 9 minutes

4 ounces sliced mushrooms
(about 1 1/2 cups)

1 medium red bell pepper, thinly sliced,
then cut in 2-inch pieces

1 cup frozen green peas, thawed

2 tablespoons no-trans-fat margarine
(35% vegetable oil)

1/4 teaspoon salt

1/8 teaspoon black pepper

1. Place a large nonstick skillet over medium-high heat until hot. Coat the skillet with nonstick cooking spray and add the mushrooms. Coat the mushrooms with nonstick cooking spray and cook 4 minutes, stirring frequently. Use two utensils to stir as you would when stir-frying.

2. Add the bell peppers and cook 2 minutes. Add the peas and cook for 1 minute.

3. Remove the skillet from the heat and stir in the remaining ingredients.

EXCHANGES / CHOICES

2 Nonstarchy Vegetable
1/2 Fat

Calories	70
Calories from Fat	25
Total Fat	3.0 g
Saturated Fat	0.6 g
Trans Fat	0.0 g
Cholesterol	0 mg
Sodium	230 mg
Potassium	220 mg
Total Carbohydrate	8 g
Dietary Fiber	3 g
Sugars	4 g
Protein	3 g
Phosphorus	65 mg

COOK'S TIP

Be careful not to overcook the peas—a minute is all they need! Otherwise they lose vibrant color and texture.

Hot Skillet Pineapple

SERVES 4 ■ SERVING SIZE 2 slices ■ PREP TIME 3 minutes
COOK TIME 7 minutes ■ STAND TIME 5 minutes

2 tablespoons no-trans-fat margarine
   (35% vegetable oil)

1 1/2 teaspoons packed dark brown sugar

1/2 teaspoon ground curry powder

8 slices pineapple packed in juice

1 Place a large nonstick skillet over medium-high heat until hot. Add the margarine, sugar, and curry and bring to a boil. Stir to blend.

2 Arrange the pineapple slices in a single layer in the skillet. Cook 6 minutes until the pineapples are richly golden in color, turning frequently.

3 Arrange the pineapples on a serving platter and let stand 5 minutes to develop flavors and cool slightly. Serve hot or room temperature.

EXCHANGES / CHOICES

1 Fruit
1/2 Fat

Calories	70
Calories from Fat	20
Total Fat	2.5 g
Saturated Fat	0.5 g
Trans Fat	0.0 g
Cholesterol	0 mg
Sodium	45 mg
Potassium	95 mg
Total Carbohydrate	13 g
Dietary Fiber	1 g
Sugars	12 g
Protein	0 g
Phosphorus	5 mg

COOK'S TIP

You'll need to buy a 20-ounce can of pineapple for this recipe (or use fresh pineapple slices from the produce aisle). It's delicious served with roasted chicken or pork.

Light Glazed Skillet Apples

SERVES 4 ■ **SERVING SIZE** 1/3 cup ■ **PREP TIME** 5 minutes ■ **COOK TIME** 5 minutes

1 tablespoon no-trans-fat margarine

1/2 tablespoon sugar

2 cups Granny Smith apple slices

1   Melt the margarine in a large skillet over medium heat, then tilt the skillet to coat the bottom evenly. Sprinkle the sugar evenly over the skillet bottom.

2   Arrange the apples in a single layer on top of the sugar. Cook 1–1 1/2 minutes or until the apples just begin to turn golden. Do not stir.

3   Using two forks or a spoon and a fork for easy handling, turn the apple slices over and cook 1 minute. Continue to cook and turn again until the apples are golden on both sides, about 2 minutes longer.

EXCHANGES / CHOICES

1/2 Fruit
1/2 Fat

Calories	45
Calories from Fat	15
Total Fat	1.5 g
Saturated Fat	0.3 g
Trans Fat	0.0 g
Cholesterol	0 mg
Sodium	20 mg
Potassium	60 mg
Total Carbohydrate	9 g
Dietary Fiber	1 g
Sugars	7 g
Protein	0 g
Phosphorus	5 mg

COOK'S TIP

These are delicious served with pork, chicken, turkey, or ham—or on your brunch table!

Crunchy Pear and Cilantro Relish

SERVES 4 ■ **SERVING SIZE** 1/4 cup ■ **PREP TIME** 6 minutes

2 firm medium pears, peeled, cored, and finely chopped (about 1/4-inch cubes)

3/4 teaspoon lime zest

3 tablespoons lime juice

1 1/4 tablespoons sugar

3 tablespoons chopped cilantro or mint

1 Place all ingredients in a bowl and toss well.

2 Serve immediately for peak flavor and texture.

EXCHANGES CHOICES

1 Fruit

Calories	50
Calories from Fat	0
Total Fat	0.0 g
Saturated Fat	0.0 g
Trans Fat	0.0 g
Cholesterol	0 mg
Sodium	0 mg
Potassium	110 mg
Total Carbohydrate	14 g
Dietary Fiber	3 g
Sugars	9 g
Protein	0 g
Phosphorus	10 mg

COOK'S TIP

If you'd like to chop the pears ahead of time, toss them with 1 tablespoon of the lime juice, then cover with plastic wrap and refrigerate up to 2 hours. At serving time, add the remaining ingredients. Try this relish with roasted pork tenderloin or baked ham.

Fruit-Scoop Muffin Cobbler
page 199

DESSERTS

Fruit-Scoop Muffin Cobbler

SERVES 8 ■ **SERVING SIZE** about 2/3 cup ■ **PREP TIME** 5 minutes
COOK TIME 1 hour and 15 minutes

1 pound frozen sliced peaches,
  partially thawed

12 ounces frozen raspberries,
  partially thawed

1 (7-ounce) package blueberry
  muffin mix (such as Martha White)

3 tablespoons canola oil

1 Preheat oven to 350°F.

2 Place the peaches and raspberries in a 13-inch
  by 9-inch baking dish coated with cooking spray.
  Sprinkle the dry muffin mix evenly over all, drizzle
  the oil over all and bake 1 hour and 15 minutes or
  until golden.

EXCHANGES / CHOICES
1 1/2 Fruit
1/2 Starch
1 Fat

Calories	160
Calories from Fat	60
Total Fat	6.0 g
Saturated Fat	0.7 g
Trans Fat	0.0 g
Cholesterol	0 mg
Sodium	120 mg
Potassium	180 mg
Total Carbohydrate	26 g
Dietary Fiber	4 g
Sugars	15 g
Protein	2 g
Phosphorus	80 mg

COOK'S TIP
This makes a great dessert, but it also makes a great
breakfast side to chicken or turkey sausage or
Canadian bacon.

Frozen Chocolate Peanut Butter Layered Pie

SERVES 8 ■ **SERVING SIZE** 1 piece ■ **PREP TIME** 8 minutes ■ **FREEZE TIME** about 4 hours

8 chocolate wafer cookies

3 1/2 cups fat-free, vanilla- or chocolate-flavored frozen yogurt or ice cream (divided use)

1/3 cup reduced-fat creamy peanut butter

2 tablespoons caramel or chocolate syrup

1 Place the cookies in a small zippered plastic bag and seal tightly. Using a meat mallet or the back of a large spoon, coarsely crush the cookies and set aside.

2 Using a fork, stir 1/2 cup frozen yogurt and the peanut butter together in a medium bowl until well blended.

3 Spoon the remaining yogurt evenly into an 8-inch pie pan. Using two spoons, drop even spoonfuls of the peanut butter mixture evenly over the yogurt.

4 Sprinkle the cookie crumbs evenly over all. Drizzle the syrup over the cookie crumbs. Cover tightly with foil and freeze until firm or at least 4 hours.

EXCHANGES / CHOICES
2 Carbohydrate
1 Fat

Calories	190
Calories from Fat	45
Total Fat	5.0 g
Saturated Fat	1.0 g
Trans Fat	0.0 g
Cholesterol	10 mg
Sodium	140 mg
Potassium	240 mg
Total Carbohydrate	29 g
Dietary Fiber	1 g
Sugars	20 g
Protein	7 g
Phosphorus	140 mg

COOK'S TIP
The yogurt and peanut butter in the second step will be a bit stiff to work with at first, but will be easier to stir as the yogurt melts slightly.

Delicate Crescent Pineapple Cake

SERVES 20 ■ **SERVING SIZE** 1 piece ■ **PREP TIME** 10 minutes ■ **COOK TIME** 33 minutes ■ **COOL TIME** 10 minutes ■ **STAND TIME** 4 hours for peak flavor

1 (18.5-ounce) box white or French vanilla cake mix

3 large eggs

1 1/3 cups water

6-ounce jar pureed pears (baby food jar)

1 (20-ounce) can sliced pineapple packed in juice, each slice cut in half (reserve juice)

1 Preheat the oven to 350°F.

2 Coat a 15 × 10-inch jellyroll pan with nonstick cooking spray and set aside.

3 Place the cake mix, eggs, water, and pears in a medium bowl and mix according to package directions. Pour the batter into the pan.

4 Arrange the pineapple halves in rows of 5 slices across and 4 slices down (creating 20 squares) and bake 33 minutes or until a wooden toothpick comes out clean.

5 Meanwhile, bring the pineapple juice to a boil in a small saucepan and continue boiling 6–7 minutes or until the liquid measures 1/4 cup. Remove the saucepan from the heat and let the juice cool.

6 When the cake has cooled 10 minutes in the pan, lightly brush the pineapple juice evenly over the cake and the pineapple slices. Cool the cake completely on a wire rack. You may serve this cake warm, but its flavors and texture are at their peak if the cake stands 4 hours. Refrigerate up to 48 hours or freeze leftovers double-wrapped with plastic wrap.

EXCHANGES / CHOICES

2 Carbohydrate

Calories	140
Calories from Fat	25
Total Fat	3.0 g
Saturated Fat	0.9 g
Trans Fat	0.0 g
Cholesterol	30 mg
Sodium	170 mg
Potassium	75 mg
Total Carbohydrate	27 g
Dietary Fiber	1 g
Sugars	17 g
Protein	2 g
Phosphorus	90 mg

COOK'S TIP

This is a great dessert to serve with grilled meat or seafood when entertaining family and friends outdoors.

Strawberries in Double-Rich Cream

SERVES 4 ▪ **SERVING SIZE** 3/4 cup ▪ **PREP TIME** 10 minutes

1 (6-ounce) container fat-free vanilla-
flavored yogurt

1 1/2 ounces reduced-fat tub-style cream
cheese

1 pint fresh strawberries, quartered

1 cup fat-free whipped topping

1 Place the yogurt and cream cheese in a blender and blend until smooth.

2 Pour the mixture into a medium bowl, add the strawberries and whipped topping, and stir gently to blend.

3 Serve immediately or cover with plastic wrap and refrigerate up to 8 hours.

EXCHANGES / CHOICES

1 1/2 Carbohydrate
1/2 Fat

Calories	140
Calories from Fat	20
Total Fat	2.5 g
Saturated Fat	1.2 g
Trans Fat	0.0 g
Cholesterol	15 mg
Sodium	95 mg
Potassium	240 mg
Total Carbohydrate	23 g
Dietary Fiber	2 g
Sugars	16 g
Protein	3 g
Phosphorus	100 mg

COOK'S TIP

Be sure to use tub-style cream cheese—it has fewer calories and less fat than the block variety.

Lemon Cream with Blueberries

SERVES 6 ■ **SERVING SIZE** 1/2 cup lemon cream with 1/3 cup blueberries ■ **PREP TIME** 5 minutes

1 (8-ounce) container fat-free whipped topping

1 cup low-fat vanilla-flavored yogurt

2 teaspoons lemon zest

3 tablespoons lemon juice

2 cups fresh or frozen unsweetened blueberries, thawed and blotted dry

1 Stir the whipped topping, yogurt, lemon zest, and juice together in a medium bowl.

2 Spoon 1/2 cup of the mixture into individual dessert bowls. Top with 1/3 cup blueberries and serve.

EXCHANGES / CHOICES
2 Carbohydrate

Calories	130
Calories from Fat	5
Total Fat	0.5 g
Saturated Fat	0.4 g
Trans Fat	0.0 g
Cholesterol	5 mg
Sodium	45 mg
Potassium	160 mg
Total Carbohydrate	26 g
Dietary Fiber	1 g
Sugars	15 g
Protein	2 g
Phosphorus	85 mg

COOK'S TIP
You can also serve this dessert frozen on a hot summer evening.

Oatmeal Cookie Apple Bowls

SERVES 8 ■ **SERVING SIZE** 1 ramekin ■ **PREP TIME** 8 minutes
COOK TIME 18 minutes ■ **STAND TIME** 10 minutes

4 cups diced Granny Smith apples (about 4 large apples), peeled (if desired)

3 tablespoons water

2 tablespoons no-trans-fat margarine (35% vegetable oil)

1/2 cup golden raisins and dried cherries

3/4 cup dry oatmeal cookie mix

1 Preheat the oven to 400°F.

2 Coat 8 (6-ounce) ramekins with nonstick cooking spray. Place 1/2 cup diced apples in each ramekin and sprinkle water evenly over each ramekin, about 1 teaspoon per ramekin.

3 Melt the margarine in a medium skillet over medium heat, then tilt the skillet to coat the bottom evenly. Remove the skillet from the heat, add the dried fruit, and sprinkle the cookie mix evenly over all. Using a fork, toss very lightly until the mixture just becomes a crumble. Do not overmix.

4 Spoon 2 rounded tablespoons of the mixture over each ramekin and bake 17 minutes, or until the crumble is just lightly golden and the apples are bubbly.

5 Remove the ramekins from the oven and let them stand 10 minutes to develop flavors. Serve warm or at room temperature.

EXCHANGES / CHOICES

2 Carbohydrate

Calories	120
Calories from Fat	20
Total Fat	2.0 g
Saturated Fat	0.3 g
Trans Fat	0.0 g
Cholesterol	0 mg
Sodium	75 mg
Potassium	150 mg
Total Carbohydrate	27 g
Dietary Fiber	2 g
Sugars	17 g
Protein	1 g
Phosphorus	40 mg

COOK'S TIP

This is delicious topped with a little fat-free vanilla ice cream or frozen yogurt.

Frozen Chocolate
Peanut Butter
Layered Pie
page 200

Popsicle Fun Pops

SERVES 12 ■ SERVING SIZE 1 pop ■ PREP TIME 15 minutes ■ FREEZE TIME 4 hours

1/2 of a 1-pound bag frozen unsweetened strawberries (about 2 cups)

1 1/2 cups white grape juice

1 cup orange juice concentrate

1 cup diet ginger ale

1 Place all ingredients in a blender and blend until smooth.

2 Pour 1/3 cup of juice into each of 12 3-ounce paper cups. Place a popsicle stick in each cup and freeze for 4 hours.

EXCHANGES / CHOICES
1 Fruit

Calories	60
Calories from Fat	0
Total Fat	0.0 g
Saturated Fat	0.0 g
Trans Fat	0.0 g
Cholesterol	0 mg
Sodium	0 mg
Potassium	230 mg
Total Carbohydrate	16 g
Dietary Fiber	1 g
Sugars	14 g
Protein	1 g
Phosphorus	20 mg

COOK'S TIP
Popsicle sticks are found in hobby stores, if your supermarket doesn't carry them.

Black Cherry–Orange Ice

SERVES 16 ■ **SERVING SIZE** 1/2 cup ■ **PREP TIME** 5 minutes ■ **FREEZE TIME** 8 hours

1 pound frozen unsweetened dark cherries

1 1/2 cups artificially sweetened cranberry juice cocktail

1 tablespoon orange zest

1/2 cup orange juice

1 tablespoon sugar

1 Place all ingredients in a blender and blend until smooth. Pour the mixture into an airtight container or a gallon-sized zippered plastic bag (release any excess air). Place in the freezer until firm, about 8 hours.

2 Using a fork, shave the frozen mixture into dessert cups. Or if you've used a zippered plastic bag, take a meat mallet or the bottom of a heavy bottle or can and crush the mixture, then place in cups.

EXCHANGES / CHOICES
1/2 Fruit

Calories	35
Calories from Fat	0
Total Fat	0.0 g
Saturated Fat	0.0 g
Trans Fat	0.0 g
Cholesterol	0 mg
Sodium	0 mg
Potassium	90 mg
Total Carbohydrate	8 g
Dietary Fiber	1 g
Sugars	6 g
Protein	0 g
Phosphorus	10 mg

COOK'S TIP
If you're not serving 16 people, you can return the unused portion of this recipe to the freezer.

Berry Peach Parfait

SERVES 4 ■ SERVING SIZE 1/2 cup ■ PREP TIME 7 minutes ■ CHILL TIME 30 minutes

1 cup water

1 (0.3-ounce) packet lemon or mixed berry sugar-free gelatin

1 cup frozen unsweetened peach slices

1 cup frozen unsweetened raspberries or blueberries

1/2 cup low-fat vanilla-flavored yogurt

1 Bring the water to boil in a small saucepan over high heat.

2 Pour the dry gelatin into a medium bowl, add boiling water to the gelatin, and stir until completely dissolved.

3 Add the frozen peaches and stir until the mixture is cold. Gently fold in the berries and stir until just blended.

4 In each of 4 parfait glasses, spoon 1/4 cup of the fruited gelatin. Top with 1 tablespoon yogurt. Repeat layers. Chill until firm, about 30 minutes, or cover with plastic wrap and refrigerate up to 24 hours.

EXCHANGES / CHOICES

1 Carbohydrate

Calories	70
Calories from Fat	5
Total Fat	0.5 g
Saturated Fat	0.3 g
Trans Fat	0.0 g
Cholesterol	0 mg
Sodium	75 mg
Potassium	210 mg
Total Carbohydrate	15 g
Dietary Fiber	1 g
Sugars	13 g
Protein	3 g
Phosphorus	90 mg

COOK'S TIP

You can boil the water in the microwave instead of on the stovetop if you prefer—it takes about 3 minutes on HIGH. Be sure to use a microwave-safe dish or measuring cup.

Double-Quick Rice Pudding

1 1/2 cups water

1/2 cup instant brown rice

3/4 cup golden raisins or other dried fruit

1 teaspoon ground cinnamon

1/8 teaspoon salt

4 (3.5-ounce) containers, ready-to-eat
   vanilla pudding

1 Bring the water to boil in a medium saucepan over high heat. Add the rice and return to a boil. Reduce the heat, cover tightly, and simmer 12 minutes. (The rice will not have absorbed all the water at this point.)

2 Remove the saucepan from the heat and stir in the dried fruit, cinnamon, and salt. Cover tightly and let stand 5 minutes.

3 Add the pudding and stir until well blended.

EXCHANGES / CHOICES
2 Carbohydrate

Calories	140
Calories from Fat	15
Total Fat	1.5 g
Saturated Fat	0.7 g
Trans Fat	0.0 g
Cholesterol	0 mg
Sodium	120 mg
Potassium	135 mg
Total Carbohydrate	30 g
Dietary Fiber	2 g
Sugars	15 g
Protein	2 g
Phosphorus	75 mg

COOK'S TIP
Don't omit the small amount of salt in this recipe—it blends the flavors together.

Creamy Tropical Freeze

SERVES 7 ■ **SERVING SIZE** 1/2 cup ■ **PREP TIME** 10 minutes ■ **FREEZE TIME** 1–4 hours

1 1/2 cups fat-free, vanilla-flavored frozen yogurt

1 pound frozen unsweetened mango or peach slices

1 ripe medium banana

1/4 cup apricot all-fruit spread

1. Place all ingredients in a blender and blend until smooth. Pour the mixture into an airtight container or a gallon-sized zippered plastic bag (release any excess air).

2. Place in the freezer for 1 hour (for a soft-serve consistency) or at least 4 hours (for a firmer dessert).

EXCHANGES / CHOICES
1 1/2 Carbohydrate

Calories	100
Calories from Fat	5
Total Fat	0.5 g
Saturated Fat	0.1 g
Trans Fat	0.0 g
Cholesterol	0 mg
Sodium	15 mg
Potassium	220 mg
Total Carbohydrate	25 g
Dietary Fiber	2 g
Sugars	20 g
Protein	1 g
Phosphorus	35 mg

COOK'S TIP
To soften slightly before serving, place this on the counter at room temperature for 10–15 minutes.

Fresh Berry and Cream Mini Tarts

SERVES 5 ■ SERVING SIZE 3 tarts ■ PREP TIME 7 minutes

1/3 cup prepared lemon curd or apricot all-fruit spread

1 (2.1-ounce) package mini phyllo shells (15 total)

1 cup fat-free whipped topping

1 cup fresh berries, such as blueberries, raspberries, or finely chopped strawberries

1 Place the lemon curd or fruit spread in a small glass bowl and microwave on HIGH for 20 seconds or until it's slightly melted.

2 Stir the mixture until smooth and spoon 1 teaspoon into each shell. Top each with 1 tablespoon whipped topping and 1 tablespoon fruit.

EXCHANGES / CHOICES

1 1/2 Carbohydrate
1/2 Fat

Calories	140
Calories from Fat	25
Total Fat	3.0 g
Saturated Fat	0.0 g
Trans Fat	0.0 g
Cholesterol	0 mg
Sodium	50 mg
Potassium	60 mg
Total Carbohydrate	26 g
Dietary Fiber	1 g
Sugars	13 g
Protein	0 g
Phosphorus	25 mg

COOK'S TIP

Lemon curd is sold in major supermarkets in the jelly and jam section.

Index

Note: Page numbers followed by *ph* refer to photographs

Soldiers of the War of 1812

**Diane Smolinski
and Henry Smolinski**

Series Consultant:
Lieutenant Colonel G.A. LoFaro

Heinemann Library
Chicago, Illinois

© 2003 Reed Educational & Professional Publishing
Published by Heinemann Library,
an imprint of Reed Educational & Professional Publishing,
Chicago, Illinois

Customer Service 888-454-2279

Visit our website at www.heinemannlibrary.com

Designed by Herman Adler Design
Photo research by Julie Laffin
Printed and bound in the United States by Lake Book
Manufacturing, Inc.

07 06 05 04 03
10 9 8 7 6 5 4 3 2 1

Library of Congress Cataloging-in-Publication Data
Smolinski, Diane, 1950-
  Soldiers of the War of 1812 / Diane Smolinski, Henry
Smolinski.
    p. cm. -- (Americans at war. The War of 1812)
Includes bibliographical references and index.
  ISBN 1-4034-0174-8
  1. United States--History--War of 1812--Juvenile literature.
2. United States--Armed Forces--History--War of 1812--
Juvenile literature. 3. Soldiers--United States--History--19th
century--Juvenile literature.
[1. United States--History--War of 1812.] I. Smolinski,
Henry. II. Title.
  E359 .S66 2002
  973.5'2--dc21
                          2002005084

Acknowledgments
The authors and publishers are grateful to the following
for permission to reproduce copyright material:
Contents page, pp. 10, 18R, 20 Anne K. S. Brown Military
Collection, Brown University Library; pp. 4, 19B, 21, 23T
The Granger Collection, New York; pp. 6, 16, 23B, 24 Mary
Evans Picture Library; p. 7 West Point Museum Collection,
United States Military Academy; p. 8B *U.S. Infantry, 1813,*
by H. Charles McBarron, Parks Canada; p. 9 Paul A.
Souders/Corbis; p. 11L National Archives of Canada;
pp. 11R, 19T North Wind Picture Archives; p. 12 Peter
Newark's Military Pictures; pp. 13, 22T, 26, 27, 28, 29
Bettmann/Corbis; p. 14 *Gunner, 3rd Regiment United States
Artillery, 1813,* by H. Charles McBarron, Parks Canada;
p. 15 *3rd Battalion, Lower Canada Select Embodied Militia,* by
G.A. Embleton, Parks Canada; p. 17 Stock Montage; p. 18L
Canadian War Museum; pp. 22B, 25 Brown Brothers.

Cover photographs: (main) The Granger Collection, New
York, (border, T-B) Corbis.

About the Authors
Diane Smolinski is the author of two previous series of
books on the Revolutionary and Civil Wars. She earned
degrees in education from Duquesne and Slippery Rock
Universities and taught in public schools for 28 years. Diane
now writes for teachers, helping them to use nonfiction
books in their classrooms. Henry Smolinski served in the
U.S. Army and U.S. Army Reserves. He earned a B.A. from
Duquesne University and has previously contributed ideas
and research for a series of books on the Revolutionary War
for young readers. Diane and Henry currently live in
Florida with their cat, Pepper.

Special thanks to Mike Carpenter for his continuing
encouragement and belief in our abilities to convey a
meaningful message to young readers.

About the Consultant
G.A. LoFaro is a lieutenant colonel in the U.S. Army
currently stationed at Fort McPherson, Georgia. After
graduating from West Point, he was commissioned in the
infantry. He has served in a variety of positions in the 82nd
Airborne Division, the Ranger Training Brigade, and
Second Infantry Division in Korea. He has a Masters
Degree in U.S. History from the University of Michigan
and is completing his Ph.D in U.S. History at the State
University of New York at Stony Brook. He has also served
six years on the West Point faculty where he taught military
history to cadets.

On the cover: This painting depicts Winfield Scott's brigade of infantry at the Battle of Chippewa, Canada, on July 5, 1814.
On the contents page: This engraving is titled "Colonel Johnson's Mounted Men Charging a Party of British and Indians at
Moravian Town, October 2, 1813." It is also known as the Battle of the Thames, which took place in Ontario, Canada.

Note to the Reader
The terms North American Indian, Indian, Indian Nation, or the specific tribe names are used here instead of Native American.
These terms are historically accurate for the time period covered in this book.

Some words are shown in bold, **like this.**
You can find out what they mean by looking in the glossary.

Contents

The War of 1812

From 1775 to 1783, American **colonists** fought to be free from British rule. This conflict is called the **Revolutionary War,** or the War of Independence, and resulted in the creation of a new nation, the United States. In 1812, problems again arose between the British and the new United States. This war is called the War of 1812, or the Second War of Independence.

Territory Report

- Thomas Jefferson was the president of the United States throughout many of the events leading up to the War of 1812. James Madison was elected president of the United States in 1809 and served as president throughout the remainder of the war.

- The King of England during the War of 1812 was George III.

British Attacks on American Shipping

United States citizens were upset that the British Navy was capturing U.S. **merchant** ships, taking their **cargo,** and kidnapping U.S. sailors. President Thomas Jefferson tried to persuade the British government to stop these unlawful attacks. His efforts proved unsuccessful. He then asked **Congress** to pass laws to stop the attacks. These laws were not able to solve the differences either.

*To keep American merchants from trading with other countries, the British Navy **blockaded** the east coast of the United States. The much smaller U.S. Navy could not stop the powerful British Navy. Here, a British naval officer boards a captured U.S. merchant ship.*

BRITISH
NORTH AMERICA

Lake Superior

MICHIGAN

Lake Huron

Mississippi River

WISCONSIN

Lake Michigan

MICHIGAN

Lake Erie

ILLINOIS

INDIANA

OHIO

Ohio River

N

0		100		200 miles
0	100		200 kilometers	

The Northwest Territory covered the area of present-day Ohio, Indiana, Illinois, Michigan, and Wisconsin. This territory held valuable natural resources such as furs, timber, and minerals.

Indian Unrest on the Western Frontier

Problems also arose between the United States and Great Britain over land on the western frontier called the **Northwest Territory.** As white settlers moved westward, they forced the Indians from these lands. The British promised to help the Indians stop the U.S. settlers from taking their land.

Declaration of War

President James Madison tried to find a peaceful solution to the problems between the U.S. and Great Britain. He, too, was unsuccessful. On June 18, 1812, Congress voted to go to war with Great Britain.

The War of 1812 would again, only 29 years later, find the United States fighting the British over international rights.

Territory Report

U.S. Territories Earn Their Statehood

When the War of 1812 began, only Ohio was a state. The other parts of the Northwest Territory were still considered territories. The dates below indicate when the territories became states.

Ohio	March 1, 1803
Indiana	December 11, 1816
Illinois	December 3, 1818
Michigan	January 26, 1837
Wisconsin	May 29, 1848

5

The U. S. Army

The U.S. Army was not prepared to fight a war in June 1812. After the **Revolutionary War** ended in 1783, most of the soldiers went home to their everyday lives. In 1812, the U.S. **Regular Army** was made up of about 6,700 soldiers. Many were not properly trained, and most of their guns and equipment were in poor condition.

Laws and Money

Congress had to act quickly to prepare the nation for war. They passed laws that allowed the size of the army to increase to 25,000 soldiers and asked the individual states to send 80,000 **militiamen.** Congress also passed laws that provided money to purchase weapons and equipment for these new soldiers.

*To get men to join the army, Congress raised the pay for privates from $5 to $8 per month, increased the **bounty** for joining from $31 to $40, and gave soldiers a three-month advance pay of $24.*

In 1802, President Thomas Jefferson signed legislation to start the United States Military Academy at West Point, a place where men could train to be officers in the U.S. Army.

Leadership

After the end of the Revolutionary War in 1783, many of the Regular Army's leaders retired. President Madison now had the task of finding new leaders to be in charge of a growing army during this time of war. Some of the leaders were trained at special military colleges, while others were appointed.

Enlisted Men

Throughout the War of 1812, many men volunteered to serve in the **infantry, artillery,** or **cavalry** units of the army. Others worked to support the troops by doing jobs such as arranging transportation for the soldiers, moving supplies, taking care of payroll, or working in the field hospitals.

Infantry Units

Most soldiers in the United States Army were part of the **infantry.**
Infantrymen generally traveled from battle to battle on foot.

Infantrymen had to carry their equipment. Some of the equipment
issued to a **Regular Army** infantry soldier during this time was:

- a **musket**—the basic weapon of the infantry;
- a **bayonet**—a long knife that attached to the end of the musket for hand-to-hand combat;
- a cartridge box—a box that held ammunition for the musket and was attached to a belt worn around the soldier's waist;
- mess equipment—a spoon, a knife, a fork, a tin cup, and a container that was used as a dish; and
- a uniform—a blue coat with a red collar, white pants, and a black **stovepipe** hat called a shako.

Since infantrymen usually marched everywhere they went, they were often called
"foot soldiers."

*Cannons similar to this coastal artillery was used to defend Fort McHenry in Baltimore Harbor, Maryland, from the attacking British **fleet.***

Field Artillery Units

Some soldiers were trained to fire and maintain cannons called **artillery.** The men, the cannons, the equipment, and the horses needed to move the cannons and equipment were called a **battery.** Field cannons helped the infantry attack enemy positions on a battlefield.

Coastal Artillery Units

Large cannons placed in or near a fort to protect a city or a **harbor** were called coastal artillery. These cannons could not be easily moved, like field artillery. They were used to keep enemy ships or troops from attacking coastal cities.

Both field and coastal artillery were important in battle because they could destroy structures that a musket could not. They could also destroy enemy forces or positions from a greater distance than what a soldier's gun could shoot.

Attacking with sabers and pistols, the cavalry was feared by the opposing infantry. The infantry was also afraid of being trampled by the charging horses' hooves.

Cavalry Units

Cavalry soldiers were trained to ride horses in battle. Cavalry units scouted ahead of the **infantry** and **artillery.** They gathered information about the opposing army's location and number of soldiers.

The cavalry would also break through an enemy battle line once the field artillery created holes in that line. Once that happened, and the enemy infantry began to flee, the cavalry would pursue them and drive them from the battlefield.

Some of the equipment used by a cavalry soldier included:
- a horse;
- a pistol—a small gun that could be fired with one hand;
- a saber—a sword with a long curved blade;
- a haversack—a strong bag used to carry a knife, fork, tin cup, and some food;
- a canteen—a container used to carry drinking water; and
- a wool blanket—used to keep warm when sleeping or riding.

Forts

Forts protected important places such as cities, rivers, **harbors,** and the borders of countries. A fort could have been one or more buildings, and were usually built of logs or stones.

Territory Report

In the 1800s, forts were important in protecting settlers from Indian attacks. For example, over 45 forts were built in the Missouri territory and another 65 were built in the Illinois territory.

Star Forts

Some of the first forts built in the United States resembled the shape of a star. Usually constructed of stone and soil, they were built to protect cities or harbors. The star design allowed the defenders of the fort to fire on enemy troops that got very close.

Stockade Forts

Forts built in the **Northwest Territories** were primarily stockade forts. The walls were made of logs placed upright in the ground. Rectangular in shape, they were more common than star forts because they were easier and quicker to build. Stockade forts most often were built to protect settlers against Indian attacks.

The layout of Fort McHenry (left) shows its five-point star shape and thick walls. The thick walls protected people inside the fort against enemy cannons. Fort Stephenson (right) was a stockade fort. Note the small windows from which soldiers inside could fire at the enemy outside.

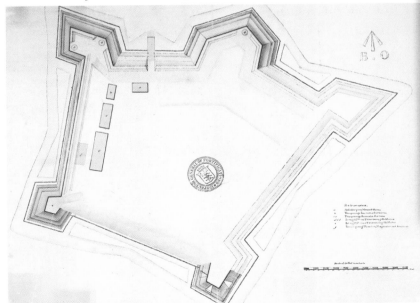

U.S. Army Leaders

Andrew Jackson
1767–1845

Before the War
Born in South Carolina in 1767, Andrew Jackson later moved to Tennessee where he became a lawyer and eventually a judge. Jackson served in the **House of Representatives** and the **Senate** for Tennessee. He resigned to become a general in the Tennessee **militia.**

During the War
As settlers moved west, Indian Nations fought to keep their lands. General Jackson defeated them in a series of battles, ending with the Battle of Horseshoe Bend. The Indians lost their land and any chance of forming a united Indian Nation.

Jackson also directed the defense of the city of New Orleans, defeating the British in 1815.

After the War
Andrew Jackson was elected the seventh president of the United States in 1828. He served for two terms, or eight years, before retiring to private life. Jackson died in June of 1845.

Andrew Jackson was well-liked by the people of the United States. He was the first elected president who did not come from a wealthy background.

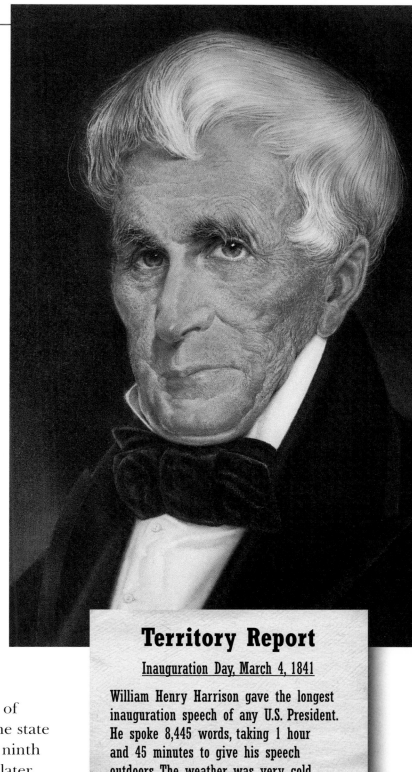

At 68 years old, Harrison was the oldest man to be elected president. After serving only 30 days in office, he died. This is the shortest term of any U.S. President.

William Henry Harrison
1773–1841

Before the War

William Henry Harrison was born in Virginia in 1773. He studied classics, history, and medicine in school. In 1791, Harrison joined the U.S. Army as an officer. He spent much of his army career fighting Indians for control of land.

During the War

In 1813, Harrison defeated the British Army and the Indian Chief Tecumseh at the Battle of the Thames, in Canada. For regaining much of the **Northwest Territory** from British control, the U.S. honored Harrison as a hero. With Tecumseh dead, the Indians no longer had a strong leader who could unite the Indian Nations.

After the War

Harrison served as a member of the House of Representatives and later as a senator for the state of Ohio. On March 4, 1841, he became the ninth president of the United States. One month later, he died of pneumonia.

Territory Report

Inauguration Day, March 4, 1841

William Henry Harrison gave the longest inauguration speech of any U.S. President. He spoke 8,445 words, taking 1 hour and 45 minutes to give his speech outdoors. The weather was very cold and windy that day.

The Militia

The American Militia

Militias were formed to protect the country against an invasion, to deal with uprisings such as riots, and to take care of other national emergencies. In April 1812, **Congress** called for 80,000 militiamen to serve in the war for a period of six months.

The Militia Act of 1792 stated who was required to serve in the militia:

…And it shall at all time hereafter be the duty of every such Captain or Commanding Officer of a company, to enroll every such citizen as aforesaid, and also those who shall, from time to time, arrive at the age of 18 years, or being at the age of 18 years, and under the age of 45 years…

The same Militia Act also explained who was not required to serve. For example, there were a few men who were exempt:

…the members of both houses of Congress… and … stage-drivers who are employed in the care…of the mail of the post office of the United States…

American militiamen were called upon to fight for the United States in the War of 1812. Many were eager to defend their new country against the British. Militiamen usually had the same uniforms within their own militias.

The Canadian militia fought on the side of the British during the War of 1812. Their uniforms and equipment were very similar to that of the U.S. militia.

In addition, the Militia Act of 1792 also described the equipment a militia soldier was to have:

…That every citizen, so enrolled and notified, shall, within six months…, provide himself with a good **musket** or firelock, a sufficient **bayonet** and belt, two spare flints, and a knapsack, a pouch, with a box therein, to contain not less than twenty-four cartridges, suited to the bore of his musket or firelock, each cartridge to contain a proper quantity of powder and ball; or with a good rifle, knapsack, shot-pouch, and powder-horn, twenty balls suited to the bore of his rifle, and a quarter of a pound of powder…

The Canadian Militia

The militia in Canada was equipped, trained, and paid in the same way as British **Regular Army** soldiers. Their main duty was to protect the British **colony** of Canada against an invasion. They also guarded prisoners, built forts, and manned British Army **outposts.**

African Americans

African Americans in the U.S. Army

African Americans were not permitted to join the U.S. Army during peacetime, but when the war started, African-American units were formed. Free African Americans volunteered to fight for the United States. Nearly 700 African Americans fought at the Battle of New Orleans during the War of 1812.

African Americans in the U.S. Navy

Many more African Americans served in the U.S. Navy during the War of 1812 than in the U.S. Army. The Navy was the first branch of the U.S. military service to allow African Americans to serve in the War of 1812. These sailors would have had duties that included working with the sails and manning the cannons.

Territory Report

African Americans Help Both Forces

- At the Battle of Lake Erie, nearly 100 of the 400 sailors in Commodore Oliver Perry's **fleet** were African Americans.

- The British welcomed slaves who wanted to escape and were willing to help the British military forces.

During the Battle of New Orleans, African Americans helped the U.S. Army defeat the British and end the war.

Women in the War

Women were not allowed to enlist in the U.S. Army during the War of 1812, but they did help with many important tasks.

Helping in Camps

On the battlefield, women removed the wounded and carried water for the soldiers. In the camps they cooked meals, did laundry, mended uniforms, and took care of injured soldiers. These women were almost always the wives of some of the soldiers in the camps.

Helping on the Home Front

Most women chose to help their country by staying home and taking care of the family business or farm. Some provided information to troops camped near their communities about the size and location of enemy troops.

One Canadian Woman

The story of Laura Ingersoll Secord is an example of one woman's courage. Laura walked nearly twenty miles (32 kilometers) to warn the British that U.S. soldiers staying in her Canadian home were planning to attack their camp.

The U.S. Army usually permitted only six women to work for each one hundred soldiers in a camp. A woman had to leave the camp or get remarried if her husband was killed in battle.

The British Army

Years of experience and better equipment made the British Army better prepared to fight a war than their U.S. opponents.

Uniforms

British soldiers wore a black **stovepipe** hat called a shako that was about eight inches (twenty centimeters) tall. U.S. soldiers sometimes called British soldiers "redcoats" because they wore short red coats with their dark blue-gray or black pants.

Weapons

Most British soldiers were armed with a **musket** called a "Brown Bess." It had a **bayonet** that could attach to the end of the barrel.

Feeding Soldiers

Each British soldier was supposed to get a six-pound (three-kilogram) loaf of bread and three quarters of a pound (one third of a kilogram) of salted meat to last him four days. The meat was dried and salted so that it would not spoil in the field.

*A well-trained British **infantryman** could fire three shots from his musket within one minute. A bayonet was attached to the end of the musket to be used as a spear in hand-to-hand combat.*

Territory Report

The musket was nicknamed the "Brown Bess" because of the great amount of time a soldier had to spend caring for it so that it would work well. A line in an English folk song states, "I'm in the King's army, married to Brown Bess."

British Army Leaders

Isaac Brock
1769–1812

Before the War

Born in 1769, Isaac Brock was the eighth son of a wealthy British family. At age fifteen, Brock entered the military and in 1810 became the commander of the entire British Army in Canada.

During the War

At the start of the war, General Brock's troops surrounded U.S. troops at Fort Detroit, causing the Americans there to surrender without a fight. He is also remembered for convincing the Shawnee Indian Chief Tecumseh to help the British fight the U.S.

General Isaac Brock was considered one of the British Army's best leaders. He was killed in the Battle of Queenston Heights in October of 1812.

When the U.S. troops, like those below, at Fort Detroit surrendered to General Brock, they actually had twice as many soldiers as the British. However, U.S. General Hull thought he was outnumbered and thus surrendered.

Sir George Prevost
1767–1816

Before the War
Sir George Prevost was born in New York City, New York in 1767, and was educated in England and North America. At age 23, he joined the British Army. In 1811, Prevost became the governor of Canada as well as the commander in chief of British forces in Canada.

During the War
General Prevost led British forces at both the Battles of Sacketts Harbor and Plattsburgh in New York. By not attacking the U.S. forces when he had the advantage, both of these battles ended in defeat for the British.

After the War
General Prevost was a good **administrator** as the governor of Canada, but he was not as successful a military leader. He was ordered to return to England to be **court-martialed,** but died in 1816 before the hearings started.

*Sir George Prevost served in several administrative posts in the **West Indies** before moving on to Canada to become governor.*

The U.S. Navy

War Begins

In 1812, the United States Navy was no match for a much larger British Navy. The U.S. Navy **fleet** was located along the east coast of the United States to protect **merchant** ships and coastal towns from attack.

Protecting the Great Lakes

At the start of the war, the U.S. Navy did not have warships on the Great Lakes to protect their border with Canada. They later rebuilt some merchant ships by adding cannons, but the British Navy still remained in control. It was not until late 1813 that the U.S. Navy gained control of these waterways.

Leadership

The U.S. Navy had officers and sailors who were experienced seamen. The more difficult task was to recruit additional sailors in great enough numbers for the ships that would be added to the Navy throughout the war.

Territory Report

Navy Pay in 1812

Navy seamen in 1812 received $10 a month. **Privateers** were also trying to recruit sailors for their own ships, so the Navy offered new recruits a signing bonus of $10 to $30 plus three months advance pay.

Getting men to join the U.S. Navy as sailors was difficult because of the low pay and the harsh living conditions.

U.S. Navy Leaders

Oliver Hazard Perry
1785–1819

Before the War
Born in Kingston, Rhode Island in 1785, Oliver Perry joined the United States Navy when he was thirteen years old. His first assignment was aboard his father's ship. In 1809 he was given command of his first ship, the USS *Revenge*.

During the War
In 1812, Perry commanded a **fleet** of twelve ships off the Rhode Island coastline. Perry found the duty boring, so he requested a transfer. He was assigned to the Great Lakes fleet. Perry's fleet of eight ships captured the entire British **squadron** in the Battle of Lake Erie in September 1813, finally giving control of the lake to the United States.

After the War
Perry continued to serve in the U.S. Navy after the war. In 1819, while on duty near Venezuela, in South America, he became ill with **yellow fever** and died.

Commodore Oliver Perry

Territory Report
Battle of Lake Erie

When the USS *Lawrence* was badly damaged as a result of British cannon fire, Commodore Perry moved his command to the USS *Niagara*. He used the *Niagara* to attack the British. Within fifteen minutes, the British surrendered. This was the first time that an entire British squadron surrendered to an American fleet.

*In the Battle of Lake Erie, Perry's **flagship,** the USS* Lawrence, *was damaged so badly that he abandoned it and rowed to the USS* Niagara.

Because of Lawrence's inexperience, the battle between the USS Chesapeake *and the* HMS Shannon *did not last long. Lawrence was defeated and died shortly after.*

James Lawrence
1781–1813

Before the War

James Lawrence was born in Burlington, New Jersey in 1781. He went away to school to study law when he was only thirteen years old, but law was not to be his life-long career. At age seventeen, he joined the U.S. Navy and first served on ships in the Mediterranean Sea, battling pirates.

During the War

In June 1813, Lawrence commanded the USS *Chesapeake*, which battled the British warship the HMS *Shannon*. Lawrence was young and inexperienced. His crew was no match for the well-trained crew of the *Shannon*. In less than one hour, the battle was over, and Captain Lawrence was seriously wounded, dying four days later.

After he was wounded, Lawrence told his men "Don't give up the ship." This saying became the motto of the U.S. Navy.

Territory Report

Lawrence's words, "don't give up the ship," were sewn onto a flag and given to Commodore Oliver Perry. Perry named his flagship the USS *Lawrence* in honor of his friend, Captain James Lawrence.

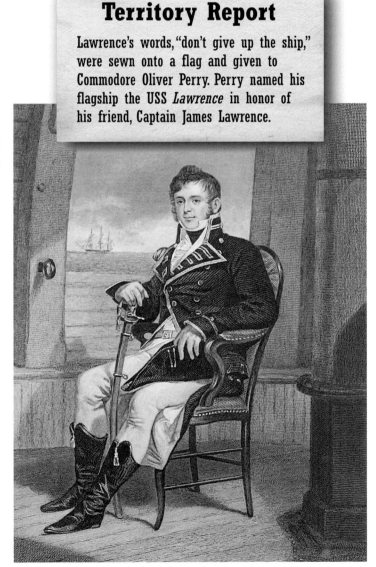

The British Navy

British Navy on the Atlantic

At the start of the war, the British **fleet** consisted of about 600 ships worldwide. Most of these ships were involved in a war that Great Britain was fighting in Europe against France. The strength of their fleet enabled them to remain in control of the Atlantic Ocean throughout the war.

British Navy on the Great Lakes

The British also had complete control of the Great Lakes and the St. Lawrence River, controlling the border between the United States and Canada. The U.S. Navy needed to defeat the British on the Great Lakes if they were to carry out their plan to invade Canada. During the last two years of the war, the U.S. Navy was successful in defeating the British on the Great Lakes.

The British fleet was responsible for patrolling over 1,500 miles (2,414 kilometers) of United States coastline.

Territory Report

Feeding the British Navy

The quality of food was often poor and sailors received the same foods week after week. A sailor's diet would include foods such as salted beef and pork, oatmeal, bread, butter, and cheese.

British Navy Leaders

Cockburn was one of the leaders responsible for converting the British fleet from sailing vessels to steam-powered ships.

George Cockburn
1772–1853

Before the War
George Cockburn was born in England in 1772. He spent the early part of his naval career on a British ship in the Mediterranean Sea. Cockburn earned the rank of admiral for being a capable leader for the British in a war against France.

During the War
In February of 1813, Cockburn arrived in the Chesapeake Bay, Maryland area. His ships raided coastal towns, destroying supplies and buildings. In 1814, Cockburn took part in the attack on Washington, D.C., when British troops set fire to the city, including the White House and **Capitol** building.

After the War
Cockburn went to the British island of St. Helena to be its governor until 1816. He then returned to England and spent the next 30 years in the British Navy. He died in 1853.

Territory Report
Napoleon Bonaparte

In 1815, George Cockburn transported the French military leader Napoleon Bonaparte to the British island of St. Helena in the Atlantic Ocean. Napoleon was taken as a prisoner to live there after suffering a defeat from years of war with many European nations.

*In the Battle of Lake Erie, Barclay had six ships compared to the U.S. with nine. His ships were not properly equipped with naval cannons, so he took cannons from a nearby fort and placed them on his **flagship**, the HMS Detroit.*

Robert Heriot Barclay
1786–1837

Before the War
Born in Scotland, Robert Barclay joined the British Navy when he was eleven years old. He was first assigned to ships that were fighting with the French during the **Napoleonic Wars.** In 1813, he was assigned to command the British **squadron** on Lake Erie.

During the War
Barclay commanded the British **fleet** on Lake Erie. In September of 1813, he was ordered to find and attack the U.S. Navy ships on Lake Erie. In the Battle of Lake Erie, the U.S. fleet defeated the British.

After the War
Because of the defeat on Lake Erie, Barclay was sent back to Great Britain to be **court-martialed.** After ten years, he cleared his name and received a promotion to captain.

Privateers

Victories by U.S. Navy ships in 1812 were important, but they were not enough to stop the British Navy from interfering with U.S. trade. Citizens thought that **privateers** could help disrupt British **merchant** shipping.

Privateers were small, fast warships that sailed mainly along the east coast of North America and in the **West Indies.** They attacked British merchant ships not protected by the British Navy and took their **cargo.** The British Navy was unable to stop them. Even though privateers inconvenienced the British, they did not affect the outcome of the war.

Territory Report

Congress needed to raise money to continue the war. U.S. Navy victories early in the war helped members of Congress convince U.S. citizens to support the war.

Most privateers were owned by businessmen or wealthy merchants only interested in making money. The men who sailed these ships were also called privateers. During the first six months of the war, privateers captured over 450 British merchant ships.

North American Indians

As settlers traveled westward, they forced the Indians from their lands. The British promised to help them stop the settlers. Most Indians, therefore, fought with the British.

Tecumseh and the Prophet

Tecumseh and his brother, called the Prophet, were Shawnee Indians who believed that Indians should be allowed to stay on their native lands. They wanted to unite all Indians into a single group, instead of fighting as individual tribes.

With defeats at the Battles of Tippecanoe and the Thames, the dream of a single Indian Nation was forever destroyed. Tecumseh was killed at the Battle of the Thames. The Indians were abandoned by the British, and forced to leave their native homelands by U.S. settlers moving westward.

Tecumseh convinced many Indians to fight on the side of the British during the War of 1812. He believed that the British would help them regain land taken by U.S. settlers. Unfortunately, when the British lost the war, the Indians were left without an ally.

Conclusion

The War of 1812 ended with the signing of the Treaty of Ghent. According to the Treaty, *Article 1:*

There shall be a firm and universal peace between His Britannic Majesty and the United States, …All hostilities, both by sea and land, shall cease as soon as this treaty shall have been ratified by both parties, …All territory, places, and possessions whatsoever, taken by either party from the other during the war, or which may be taken after the signing of this treaty, …shall be restored without delay.

Many Americans, British, and Indians lost their lives in this war. The war ended without solving most of the problems that caused it, including the dispute over land in the **Northwest Territory** and the British harassment of U.S. shipping.

After the attack on Fort McHenry in 1814, Francis Scott Key saw the American flag still flying over the fort and wrote a poem about what he saw. This poem, "The Star Spangled Banner," later became our National Anthem.

*…And the star-spangled banner
in triumph shall wave
O'er the land of the free and the home of
the brave.*

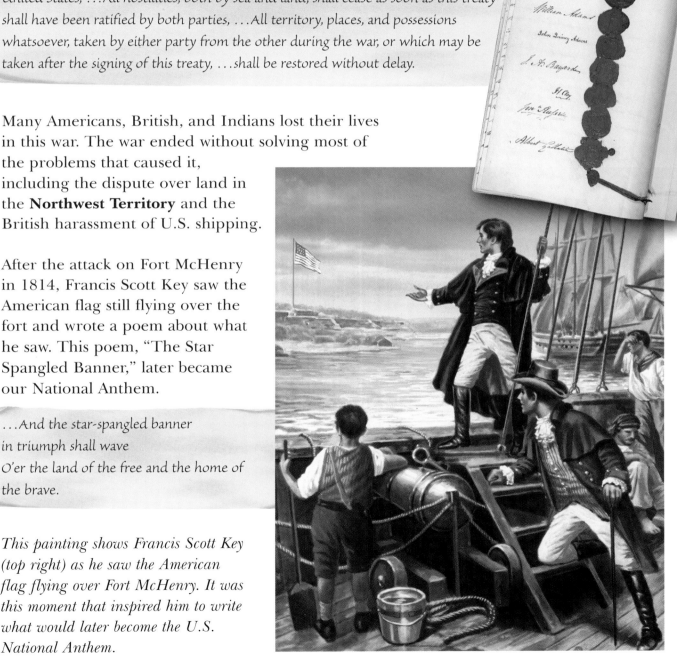

This painting shows Francis Scott Key (top right) as he saw the American flag flying over Fort McHenry. It was this moment that inspired him to write what would later become the U.S. National Anthem.

Glossary

administrator   person in charge of a business, school, or government affairs

artillery   cannons

battery   artillery unit of men, cannons, equipment, and horses

bayonet   long, pointed knife that attached to the end of a musket

blockade   troops or warships that block enemy troops or supplies from entering or leaving an area

bounty   reward

Capitol   building in which the U.S. Congress meets in Washington, D.C.

cargo   goods carried by a ship for trading

cavalry   soldiers who rode horses

colony   territory settled by people from other countries who still had loyalty to those other countries. The word *colonist* is used to describe a person who lives in a colony.

Congress   men who represented the individual states in the U.S. government, either in the House of Representatives or the Senate

court-martial   to convict by a special military court

flagship   ship that the leader of a group of ships sails on

fleet   group of ships

harbor   place along the coastline that provides protection for ships

House of Representatives   group of elected leaders that make laws for all U.S. citizens

infantry   foot soldiers

merchant   ship that carries goods for trading, or a person who buys and sells goods

militia   small military unit of ordinary men organized by an individual state. Men who fought in the militia were called *militiamen*.

musket   gun with a long barrel carried by the infantry

Napoleonic Wars   series of wars that Napoleon Bonaparte of France fought against much of Europe between 1800 and 1815

Northwest Territory   land that covered the present-day states of Ohio, Michigan, Illinois, Indiana, and Wisconsin

outpost   small military fort

privateer   small, fast warship used to disrupt British merchant shipping. The men who sailed on these ships were also known as privateers.

regular army   full-time soldiers

Revolutionary War   American fight for independence from British rule between 1775–1783

Senate   group of elected leaders that make laws for all U.S. citizens

squadron   part of a larger group of ships

stovepipe   tall hat

West Indies   group of islands between North and South America

yellow fever   tropical disease carried by a mosquito

Historical Fiction to Read

Buckey, Sarah Masters. *The Smuggler's Treasure (American Girl History Mysteries Series #1).* Middleton, Wis.: Pleasant Company, 1999.
In New Orleans during the War of 1812, an eleven-year-old girl is determined to find a pirate's treasure to use as ransom for her imprisoned father.

Gillem, Harriette and Robinet Gillem. *Washington City is Burning.* New York: Simon and Schuster, 1996.
A slave in the White House experiences the burning of Washington, D.C. by the British in Virginia in 1814 during the War of 1812.

Minahan, John A. *Abigail's Drum.* New York: Pippin Press, 1995.
Based on an actual event during the War of 1812, two young daughters of the local lighthouse keeper in a Massachusetts town figure out a way to save him and the town when British soldiers kidnap their father.

Historical Places to Visit

Fort McHenry National Monument and Historic Shrine
East Fort Avenue
Baltimore, Maryland 21230-5393
Visitor information: (410) 962-4290
Three miles southeast of the Baltimore Inner Harbor, this park's visitor center houses exhibits, a model of the star fort, an electric battle map, and a theater where an orientation film, "The Defense of Fort McHenry," is shown. Take a self-guided tour of the star fort, statues, cannons, and restored barracks. This battle site inspired Francis Scott Key to write the poem, "The Star-Spangled Banner," which became the National Anthem of the United States.

Fort George
Niagara National Historic Sites
Box 787, 26 Queen Street
Niagara-on-the-Lake, Ontario L0S IJ0
Canada
Visitor information: (905) 468-4257
Dressed in uniforms of the time period, reenactors perform activities typical to life in and around the fort just before the start of the War of 1812. Soldiers practice drilling and a fife and drum corps play music from the time period.

Fort Mackinac
P.O. Box 370
Mackinac Island, Michigan 49757
Visitor information: (906) 847-3328 or (231) 436-4100
Constructed by British soldiers during the Revolutionary War, Fort Mackinac served as a lookout in the Straits of Mackinac. Tour some of the original fort buildings and exhibits of military life from the War of 1812. Musket demonstrations, cannon firings, and tours by costumed guides are just some of the many activities taking place at the fort.

Index